I0142080

YOUR BRILLIANT MIND:

WONDERFUL SERVANT OR WICKED MASTER?

An ordinary person's story and guide to overcoming physical and psychological pain.

JAMES GARRETT

Silent River Publishing, LLC

PUBLISHER'S NOTE

The information in this book is meant to supplement, not replace, the services of qualified healthcare or mental health professionals. It should not be used to diagnose or treat any specific illness or patient. Neither the author nor the publisher offers professional advice or services to readers. If you have concerns about your physical health or mental well-being, please consult your healthcare or mental health provider.

All references to the Bible are from the King James Version unless otherwise specified.

Silent River Publishing, LLC

Copyright© 2025 by James Garrett

Silent River Publishing, LLC
#1188
1201 Kings Highway STE 2
Fairfield, CT 06824

All rights reserved.
Cover and interior design by HMD Publishing.
Edited by Judith Kern and Aya Summers.

To my wife, whose grace steadies me, and to my youngest son Ayden, whose extraordinary light turned my world upside down and illuminated the path to these pages—this book exists because of you.

CONTENTS

PREFACE

It was nearly midnight, and I was wide awake. The next day marked the start of a new school year, and I struggled to fall asleep. Even as a young child, I understood what the problem was—I couldn't stop thinking. To help myself drift off, I played a simple game I had invented called "The Mental Chalkboard."

I've always been a visual thinker, so when I couldn't sleep, I pictured my thoughts appearing on a vast chalkboard. Next, I'd take an imaginary eraser and wipe away each thought. Often, this made the thoughts reappear elsewhere on the chalkboard, leading me to erase them multiple times until I had a clean slate. Then, I would scan the chalkboard for any lingering thoughts to erase until I finally fell asleep. This process resembled the whack-a-mole arcade game but used an eraser instead of a hammer. I continued this method whenever I had trouble sleeping, well into adulthood, and it usually helped me fall asleep within ten minutes.

Falling asleep and staying asleep became significant issues later in life when I began struggling with chronic physical pain and anxiety. My anxiety stemmed from raising a violent teenager with a rare genetic disorder, caring for an elderly parent with dementia, and trying to support two other children through college—all at the same time. I suspected that my physical pain and anxiety were connected because I had experienced some mind-body symptoms in my younger years and had seen several doctors who were unable to help me. When my condition escalated to the point where I could not sleep at all and was having trouble functioning, I started reading self-help books in search of a solution.

One of the popular books I picked up was Eckhart Tolle's *The Power of Now*. Early in the book, Tolle introduced a radical idea that I will never forget—he suggested that we are not our thoughts.[1] As a successful design engineer who values thinking, I dismissed his book as nonsense and set it aside.

A short time later, when I found myself lying awake once again from physical pain and anxiety, I decided to play "The Mental Chalkboard" game to help me fall asleep. As I began playing, a curious question occurred to me: *Who is doing the erasing, and who is putting the thoughts on the chalkboard?* I realized that they couldn't both be me, and the one putting the thoughts on the chalkboard was certainly not me. Whoever he was, I didn't want him in charge. I returned to Tolle's book, and the idea that I was not my thoughts started to make sense. That moment of awareness pointed me in the right direction and marked the beginning of a long journey.

Following this realization, I delved into numerous books on psychosomatic pain, cognitive behavioral therapy (CBT), and spiritual growth. At first, I felt overwhelmed by the wealth of information and the diverse practices presented in these texts. However, one technique that particularly stood out to me was expressive writing. This practice involves jotting down your thoughts and feelings on paper for a few minutes each day and then tearing them up. The goal is to help you separate from repetitive and negative thoughts and feelings. Unlike other methods I had tried for calming the mind, I found that I could engage in this practice even while experiencing severe back pain, neck pain, and a range of other symptoms. I began scribbling down my thoughts and feelings daily, and within a few weeks, I noticed a gradual reduction in my pain, which motivated me to continue with the practice.

After practicing for months and making further improvements, I noticed a peculiar space that had developed between my emotions and me. I still experienced anxiety and some anger, *but it felt as if I were observing these feelings in someone else,* which made them less

_____

1. Tolle, The Power of Now, p 11

bothersome. This experience was both strange and wonderful—leading me to realize that I was onto something significant.

Another practice that stood out to me in my reading was surrender. Surrender is difficult to define concisely, yet it is a profoundly powerful concept. This book will explore surrender in depth, discussing its meaning and how to practice it. Learning and practicing surrender took me deeper into my spiritual journey and empowered me to quell specific negative thoughts and feelings, which is a step beyond merely separating from them.

Six months after I began these practices, my physical pain had largely disappeared—including symptoms that had lasted for over twenty years. These symptoms included chronic lower back pain, neck pain, tendonitis, neuropathy in my hands and feet, difficulty swallowing, and more. Even pain from an old injury, which I never linked to mental stress, unexpectedly faded away. Although I still felt some anxiety and anger, I was gradually learning to distance myself from these emotions. At that time, I found it difficult to comprehend how any of this was possible and could hardly believe what had happened to me. Eventually, I realized how closely the mind and body are interconnected.

A deeper sense of freedom from anxiety and anger emerged later, after I explored the diverse concepts in psychology and spiritual growth that I had been studying. Initially, these ideas seemed contradictory, but I eventually saw how they harmonized beautifully. Cognitive behavioral therapy (CBT) taught me to recognize ten different cognitive distortions that occur in the mind, which stand at the root of most anxiety and some forms of depression. Once I became aware of these distortions, I learned to quiet my mind by focusing on my inner body and observing my emotions without attaching any stories to them. Through this practice, I learned the hard truth about emotional pain—*you must experience it to be free from it*. Eventually, my inner space became very still as I continued practicing these and other concepts you'll read about in this book.

Contrary to what I've been taught in churches throughout my life, I've discovered that a quiet mind is not a foreign, unnatural, or precarious state. Instead, it is the natural result of releasing worries, fears, judgments, attachments, the past, and other negative and repetitive thoughts. I found that the practice of mental stillness, also known as meditation, is not dangerous—it is simply about separating from useless and harmful thoughts, instead of allowing the world and past conditioning to dictate them. Unfortunately, the practice of quieting the mind is seldom taught in churches or schools, despite the Psalmist's admonition to *"Be still, and know that I am God."*[2] I hope this book will help to change that—in hindsight, I can't imagine anything more important.

Emotional pain can hurt more than physical pain, and this book is about finding freedom from both. I'm not a doctor, therapist, or psychologist—I'm just an ordinary guy who found freedom from pain after years of suffering, and I want to share what I have learned.

Psychology and spirituality are deeply connected because grace cannot flow into your life when your psyche is tangled in knots. Grace began to flow when I learned to be mentally still, and in that stillness, I discovered a new awareness of the ineffable beneath the mental noise.

---

2. Ps 46:10

INTRODUCTION

The human mind is a complex computing instrument with endless imaginative powers and an immense memory that records everything in three-dimensional color and sound. It can perform tasks that surpass the world's most powerful supercomputers. However, how do we use this incredible tool? Too often, we replay painful memories from the past and worry about an imagined future. This constitutes a tragic misuse of our minds, akin to using a violin to pound nails instead of creating beautiful music.

The average person has thousands of thoughts each day, many of which are repetitive and negative. Often, these thoughts can be irrational, harmful, or a constant drain on mental and emotional energy. They may include worries, insecurities, attachments, judgments, compulsions, resentment, guilt, and more. If you take a moment to reflect on these thoughts, you will notice that many arise automatically and are beyond your control.

Human beings possess a lower nature similar to that of animals, yet we also have a higher self that grants us the unique ability to choose how we think and respond. This lower nature is known by many names, including the ego, the false self, the natural man, the carnal mind, and the sinful nature. Although these terms may have distinct meanings, they all convey a common theme: the condition where the mind has taken control, leaving the true you—the higher self—no longer in charge.

Psychology aims to understand and manage the mind, while spirituality seeks to transcend it. It does this by teaching us to connect with the true self that is aware of the many levels of our being, including thoughts and emotions. Rather than being in conflict, psychology and spirituality complement each other. A century of psychological research has increased awareness of mental dysfunction, enabling you—the true self—to recognize distorted thoughts and learn to separate from them.

Many people associate spiritual growth with having faith and obeying commandments; however, it also includes introspection, which is the examination of one's mental and emotional processes. Spiritual growth entails learning to recognize dysfunctional thinking and observing it without being controlled by it; almost like being the sky and watching the weather pass through. It means breaking free from the shackles of negative thoughts and viewing life not as a problem, but as an opportunity to grow by responding to life from an empowered place, rather than merely reacting to it from a triggered reflex.

Reactions are inevitable when you identify with your thoughts and feelings, but a spiritual person learns to *disidentify* from them, so they are not controlled by them. Learning to disidentify is a process that requires effort and is achieved through introspection, practicing mental stillness, and continually asking the question, "Who am I?" These practices foster awareness and recognition that thoughts and feelings are not the essence of who you are, just as your body is not the essence of who you are. This is not a doctrine to believe in—it is known experientially through introspection and practice.

When you look inward and notice your thoughts, you see that they come and go like the wind, but *you* are always there observing them. When you notice an unpleasant thought, you see that your natural tendency is to push it away. But then you realize the thought you're pushing away cannot be *you*, because you're the one doing the pushing. When you notice a pleasant thought, you see that your natural tendency is to cling to it. But then you realize the thought you're clinging to cannot be *you*, because *you* are the one who is doing the clinging.

As you reflect inward, you will notice that one moment you feel sad, the next moment you feel happy, and still another, you may feel angry. However, it is always the same *you* experiencing these ever-changing emotions. Thoughts and feelings are fleeting, but *you* are the ever-present awareness or consciousness behind them. *You* are the true self, whose essence cannot be fully captured in words.

If you are skeptical that your thoughts and feelings are not your true self, consider this—try to forgive someone purely with your mind, and you will likely find it impossible. Your brilliant mind is incredibly skilled at justifying and rationalizing nearly any thought, feeling, or behavior. It will constantly seek to prove that it is right and that others are wrong, often finding new ways to assign blame. Ultimately, the mind cannot forgive—only *you* can forgive. True forgiveness requires the cessation of thinking. *You* must choose to stop thinking about the situation and let go of those thoughts and feelings.

Your true self is the one that makes conscious choices, and you can choose to gently take control of your mind. Taking control of your mind is like driving a car; you determine its direction, when it moves, and when it stays parked. This practice not only enhances *your* well-being but also has a positive impact on those around you.

If you don't take charge of your brilliant mind, it will run on autopilot, filling your head with the voices of worry, discontent, and the replaying of past pains. The voice in your head can be irrational at times, and it can significantly affect your mood, actions, and overall ability to function if you don't learn to control it. Automatic thoughts can be toxic and will ultimately harm you, your relationships, and may even lead to physical pain.

Although the voice in your head can be irrational, spirituality is in fact, quite rational. Spirituality involves navigating reality by letting go of unconstructive, repetitive, and erroneous thoughts. It also involves releasing attachments to material things, as it's a *fact* that you can't take them with you. Feelings are not *facts*, and while emotions add richness and depth to life, a spiritual person understands that they can fool you and lead to unnecessary suffering. Spirituality directs your attention to the present moment because this is where your entire life unfolds. If your thoughts are fixated on the past or the future, you are essentially missing out on your life.

Automatic thoughts and feelings, such as worry and anxiety, are pervasive, yet little is taught in schools or churches about how to escape them. Fortunately, this knowledge is available in many spiritual traditions and modern psychology. Both disciplines teach that you cannot fight negative thoughts and feelings—doing so will only strengthen them. True freedom begins with becoming aware of what's happening inside and learning to be comfortable with all your feelings instead of pushing them away. As you become more comfortable with negative thoughts and feelings, they diminish and lose their intensity.

Negative feelings want to be fed like hungry animals seeking food. We feed them by replaying mental stories, movies, narratives, and engaging in two-way mental conversations. I live in New England, where wild Canadian Geese have overrun some of our parks. The geese come to our parks and linger because people feed them. While it's natural to want to feed them, this creates a nuisance and attracts even more geese. Over time, a beautiful park can turn into a very unpleasant place. The geese are like automatic negative feelings, such as anger and anxiety. When you experience these feelings, it's natural to want to feed and strengthen them with a story, such as how somebody wronged you in the past or the possibility that something terrible might occur in the future. However, replaying these stories will cause the feelings to persist and ultimately create an emotional mess within you. *The solution is to let go of the mental stories and allow the feelings to be.*

I use the terms "feelings" and "emotions" interchangeably to describe bodily sensations that are linked to thoughts, and this connection resembles that of thunder and lightning. Feelings, or emotions, are the energies generated by thoughts that resonate throughout your body, just as thunder echoes after lightning. However, there are times when you may feel gloomy or anxious, but the thoughts that trigger these feelings may not be immediately apparent, much like hearing distant thunder without seeing the lightning. Emotional energy, like thunder, can be powerful and seeks to be released. The best way to achieve this is to allow yourself to relax into those feelings instead of trying to push them away.

This concept is known as "*leaning into the pain.*" It involves actively paying attention to unpleasant emotional sensations in your body without attaching mental narratives to them. By letting go of the mental stories, you can relax, as constant thinking tends to create tension. Essentially, the approach to managing uncomfortable feelings is the same as managing pleasant ones—welcome them and allow them to be, instead of fighting or suppressing them. This enables you to experience emotional energy so it can flow through you. The practice of *"leaning into the pain"* helps create space or separation between you and the uncomfortable feelings while simultaneously helping to dissolve those feelings.

When you separate from the feeling of anxiety, it becomes like a flock of noisy birds flying over your head. You are aware of the birds, but they cannot build a nest in your hair. The birds will do what birds do, but you won't mind them. Remember, birds don't stick around forever—eventually, they will fly away.

When you separate yourself from the feeling of anger, it's similar to watching a storm through a window while sitting comfortably at home. The storm may rage outside with cold winds and rain, but you remain unaffected because you are warm and safe indoors. Storms do not last forever—eventually, the clouds will clear, and the sunshine will return.

When you begin to separate yourself from the feeling of depression, you will start to say, "There is depression" instead of "I am depressed." You can allow the dark, heavy feeling to be there without identifying with it, recognizing that it does not define who you are. *It's as if you are observing the depression in someone else, and it loses its power over you.*

Finding this space or separation is known as dis-identification, which means the unpleasant feeling no longer has a grip on you. Instead, you are "the watcher" of it. Being the "silent observer" means not feeding the feeling with a story, but watching it pass through you and eventually dissolve. Anyone can learn how to do this, and it does not require special talent—but it *does* require regular practice. This book is about how to develop that practice.

Negative feelings such as anxiety, resentment, and guilt can be likened to emotional trash that no longer serves you. New England has limited space for traditional landfills, so we no longer bury and cover all of our trash. Instead, most household waste is transformed into clean electricity at efficient trash-to-energy facilities. Similarly, we all carry emotional trash from past experiences that trigger automatic negative thoughts. However, instead of burying this emotional trash, you can learn to transform it into positive energy, such as enthusiasm, if you're willing to lean into it and become comfortable with it. This is why individuals with the most challenging pasts often undergo the most dramatic transformations. The more difficult your past, the more fuel you have to foster growth, and the brighter your light will shine—*if* you have the courage to engage in the alchemical process.

To understand this process, we must first understand how emotions and thoughts, which are energy, can manifest in the body as physical symptoms. This idea might seem like a stretch and is often dismissed as "snake oil." However, medical science is gradually starting to recognize it as a legitimate phenomenon—known as mind-body syndrome (MBS), tension myositis syndrome (TMS), psychophysiological disorder (PPD), neurophysiologic disorder (NPD), or simply psychosomatic pain. Most people understand that stressful thoughts can lead to tension headaches, which is an experience many have had. So, it raises the question—why couldn't chronic mental stress lead to a persistent backache or other forms of chronic pain?

When asked to give a speech in front of a large audience, you may notice various physical sensations and changes in your body. Your hands and feet may feel cold, often called "cold feet," as blood flow to your extremities decreases. You may also feel slight nausea, commonly described as having "butterflies in your stomach." You may rush to the restroom because your bowels may feel the urge to empty. Your heart might race, your hands shake, and you may sweat. You may stammer when speaking, and your breathing may become shallow, causing you to gasp for air. Clearly, thoughts about public speaking can influence many parts of the body.

Should it be surprising, then, that recurring anxiety or anger can sometimes manifest as chronic physical conditions? My personal story is a prime example of how this can and does happen, but not everyone will have the same experience. Many people suffer from deep anxiety and anger without experiencing physical pain. Everyone is wired a bit differently, but at the end of the day, we all want to be free from both physical and emotional pain.

Chronic pain is not just an academic topic for me—it's a deeply personal experience. I endured many years of severe migraine headaches, chronic lower back pain, chronic neck pain, chronic tendonitis in my joints, hand and foot neuropathy, temporomandibular disorder, prostatitis, difficulty swallowing, and more. However, the most debilitating pain I faced was anxiety, which felt like a slow poison. After years of suffering, I am relieved to say that all this pain is now gone. I understand the skepticism that many people have regarding psychosomatic pain. My escape from physical pain was so remarkable and unexpected that I can hardly believe it myself now.

Science, however, confirms that repetitive negative thoughts *can* contribute to—or be the cause of—chronic physical pain. It has also been shown that physical pain and emotional pain are processed in similar areas of the brain, and in many ways, they are equivalent.[3] Freedom from both is found by becoming a "silent observer" and learning to be comfortable with negative thoughts and feelings without feeding them with mental narratives. You can learn to welcome uncomfortable feelings just as you welcome good feelings—a practice known as non-resistance. When your thoughts and emotions start to overwhelm you, your task is always to relax and let them be. Don't feed them with more stories, don't push them away, and don't try to change them. This does not come naturally to most people, but we'll delve deeply into how to do it.

The mind doesn't just create suffering through *negative* thoughts—it can also use *positive* thoughts. I practiced positive thinking for decades—this left my body a train wreck. While positive thinking has its value and feels good, it is often used to suppress negative thoughts and feelings. Unfortunately, the more you try to push a negative thought away, the stronger it becomes, making it more likely to return and bother you repeatedly. Suppressing thoughts can also drain your energy, leading to more suffering. The path to freedom lies in silently observing your thoughts and emotions instead of trying to ignore them.

---

3. Hanscom, Back in Control, p 20

When you learn to do this, your mind will gradually settle down—allowing you to enter a state of rest that transcends positive thinking.

Anger and anxiety are often at the root of chronic physical pain, but some anger is normal and healthy when it doesn't linger for long periods. In a spiritually mature person, healthy anger can lead to positive action; however, it has a very short life and moves through them quickly because it's not being resisted or fed. When you learn to relax and allow anger to pass through you, it loses its power to create chronic physical pain. It's not necessary to rid yourself of all anger and anxiety for this to happen; in my case, only a small change was needed for the physical pain to begin resolving. As you will see, doing one simple practice each day will yield results quickly.

Pain and suffering are not the same. Pain is a physical sensation felt in the body, while suffering is the mind's reaction to that sensation. When we suffer, we often fixate on repetitive thoughts, such as "When will this end?", "Why is this happening to me?", "I don't deserve this," and "I can't take this anymore." Although pain can sometimes be unavoidable, suffering is a choice we make. Later, we will explore how the repetitive stories and scripts we associate with the sensations of pain can cause those sensations to be amplified and memorized by our nervous system.

If you are experiencing chronic physical pain, you should see your doctor; however, be aware that it is unlikely that he or she will suggest that your way of thinking is the cause. Ultimately, you must take responsibility for your care. You are unique because you have inside information on one person—that person is you. You know more about your thoughts and feelings than anyone else on the planet. While it can be helpful to work with a therapist or healthcare professional, if you want to be free of pain, you must take an active role in your healing. No one else can do this for you—you must do the work yourself.

Working on yourself means focusing on the inner self, as all human experiences occur internally. All the external information your five senses gather is processed within. *Every ounce of peace, joy, happiness, and love you've ever felt, happened internally rather than externally.* Therefore, your primary task is to mend what's broken inside; your secondary task is to address what's necessary outside. Mending the inside means learning to disidentify from useless, negative, and repetitive mental chatter. When you fix what's broken inside, external situations often resolve with less effort. Your ability to change the outside world is limited—but there are no limits to the changes you can make within.

If you do the inner work, you can feel good at any time, no matter what's happening outside. The outside world has ten thousand problems waiting in line to bother you—and this line will always be there. You can joyfully participate in every situation, even the difficult ones, by doing what's necessary instead of merely reacting. You can choose not to give anyone, anything, or any situation the privilege of upsetting you. Learning to do this takes effort, but it doesn't require any special talent or skill. It only requires a desire to be free from enslavement to the mind.

When you're no longer a slave to automatic thoughts and emotions, you will abide in a place of rest with newfound clarity and enthusiasm. When your inner space is free from useless and harmful mental and emotional noise, you can use your brilliant mind to serve others and address whatever life throws your way. Life transforms into an adventure—rather than just a series of problems.

The first one-third of this book (chapters 1-7) shares my long journey through pain and how I ultimately found freedom from it. The remaining chapters (chapters 8-25) are more prescriptive, focusing on increasing awareness of the dysfunctional thinking that causes pain and providing guidance on how to break free from it.

Chapter 1

MY JOURNEY INTO PAIN

The first ten years of my life were spent just outside Boston in a neighborhood where all the homes were very close together, so everyone knew each other. I had a close-knit group of friends, an older brother, and a younger sister. I never felt alone because there was always someone around to play with. I could hop on my bike at any time and find a friend to ride with, go fishing, play wiffleball or street hockey, build a go-kart, or just hang out. I did well in school and was very conscientious. I was happy and always giggling about something—my nickname was "giggling boy." My parents were very loving and attentive, and I cannot recall a single moment of fear, anxiety, or sadness during those ten years.

One of the joys of being a kid in the 1970s was the walk to school, which was about two miles from home. Our path took us through the woods along a winding river, where my friends and I explored and looked for snapping turtles and other creatures. We arrived at school feeling energized from the walk and often played kickball in the schoolyard before class started. The walk home was just as enjoyable, and after arriving home, we would frequently grab our fishing poles and head back to the river.

I enjoyed going to school because it was always associated with fun and adventure. During those years, homework wasn't assigned until the sixth grade, so there was never any concern about assignments interfering with our playtime.

The river was a wonderful place for fishing and exploring, and I spent many hours there whenever I could. However, the water was polluted, with signs warning that it was unsafe to eat the fish or even swim. Despite this, the river was teeming with large fish that didn't seem to be affected. We had three favorite fishing spots: the bridge, the sandbar, and the dock. The bridge was situated in a wide, open area with no trees, while the other spots were nestled in dense woods and shaded areas.

One sunny day, after fishing at the bridge, I came home with a terrible headache and felt sick. My mother suggested I must have caught a "bug," but I felt fine the next day. This happened several times, and I began to notice a pattern: fishing at the bright, sunny bridge often resulted in me coming home ill with this mysterious "bug." As a result, I preferred the shadier sandbar and dock, even though they weren't the best spots for fishing.

In hindsight, it's clear that I began experiencing occasional migraine headaches around the age of eight. The sun's glare reflecting off the water seemed to trigger them, which is common among migraine sufferers. However, at that time, I didn't understand what was happening, and none of my friends experienced similar issues. Many years later, I learned that both my parents, my maternal grandparents, and most of my aunts and cousins also suffered from migraines, indicating that I had inherited a strong genetic predisposition.

One day, when I was ten, I overheard my parents discussing the possibility of moving out of state. The thought scared me, and I felt too anxious to ask about it, hoping the topic would fade away. However, my parents had relatives living out of state, and my grandfather on my mother's side had offered them land to build a house.

Before I knew it, we were no longer just discussing the idea—we were moving. This was a personal crisis for me, and I expressed my objections loudly. My older brother and younger sister shared my feelings. Despite our parents' assurances that we would be relocating to the countryside, with its open spaces and great opportunities, I was overwhelmed with fear. I felt like I was losing everything I knew and loved.

The new house was located in a rural area, where the homes were quite far apart, and very few children our age lived within a mile in any direction. There were no nearby fishing spots, and the road in front of our house was unsafe for street sports or go-karts. We moved in October, so the school year had already begun. My siblings and I were given just one day to settle in before starting school, and since it was too far to walk, we needed to take the bus.

Everyone at the new school was friendly—but everything felt different. I was in fifth grade, and while at my old school, girls were still considered "poison" at that age, here, they were viewed as interesting, which felt strange to me. I had never encountered a male elementary school teacher before; however, many of the teachers here were men.

My new male teacher was very strict and enforced specific rules, such as requiring students to put their chairs on their desks at the end of each day. If someone failed to do this, they would be assigned to write "I will put my chair up each day" one hundred times. This number would double for each day the assignment was not completed. Homework was assigned daily and was expected to be done the next day. I had never taken a book home from school before and resented the stack of books I now had to carry.

I felt unwell upon arriving home at the end of the first day. My head was pounding, and I was vomiting as I staggered into our new house. My parents were convinced I had caught yet another "bug" and thought I would need to stay home the next day. However, I felt perfectly fine the following morning, with no fever or other symptoms. Since I hadn't completed my homework, I asked my parents for a note, fearing that I would receive an assignment for not doing it.

The second day mirrored the first. I came home feeling very unwell and almost vomited on the school bus. My parents were puzzled, but I felt okay again the next morning. This pattern continued each day for the first week but gradually subsided.

After moving, I felt like a different person, and migraine headaches became a regular occurrence. However, at that time, most people didn't believe children could have migraines, so they never considered that I might be experiencing them. I was no longer giggling all the time—instead, I had become very quiet. My parents could see my tension as I headed off to school each morning and advised me to "loosen up"— their advice didn't help. I was going through a lot of emotional pain, including anxiety, and I felt lost and deeply sad. I remember being on the verge of tears much of the time I was at school, but I was too embarrassed to talk about it with anyone.

School, which was once a source of joy for many years, had turned into a place of constant dread and anxiety. I felt as if I had lost my whole world, and it hurt. All my close friends were suddenly gone, and I knew I would never see them again. My afternoons, once spent fishing and biking, were now spent alone in my room doing homework. Those dark feelings about school and losing my friends lingered into sixth grade, and it felt like a never-ending nightmare.

Eventually, I made some great new friends, but I always felt like an outsider. That feeling lingered into adulthood. Back then, it wasn't something I could discuss, so I pushed through while maintaining a calm and quiet demeanor.

Experiencing migraines during the first few days of school became a recurring pattern for me, continuing through college and even on my first day at a new job. At that time, there were no effective rescue medications like Sumatriptan, which has since been a lifesaver for many. My only options were to take aspirin and wait it out while lying in a dark room with an ice pack on my head. Eventually, I discovered that vigorous aerobic exercise in the early stages of a migraine could sometimes halt its progression, so I often found myself running outdoors, sometimes even in the middle of the night.

Stress was the main trigger for most of my migraines, but there were also other, less common causes. Over the years, I gradually learned that certain foods could contribute to my condition, so I carefully avoided chocolate, artificial sweeteners, and most tropical fruits. Additional triggers included sun glare, irregular sleep patterns, and intense physical activity in hot weather.

It's hard to truly explain what a severe migraine feels like to someone who has never experienced one. Besides a pounding head, it's like having the stomach flu, with symptoms of vomiting, fatigue, and depression. They often come with partial vision loss—almost as if you've been hit in the head with a baseball bat. In those moments, you feel as if you want to die. I wouldn't wish this condition on anyone;

however, as we'll see later, our greatest strength often emerges from our weaknesses.

I learned to expect migraines in certain situations. I could feel my heart pounding and adrenaline rushing as I entered a new classroom or job site for the first time, and this would inevitably trigger a migraine. This reaction had somehow become programmed in me—no matter how hard I tried to relax, my emotions would go into autopilot, producing waves of anxiety.

Strangely, people often remarked, "Jim, you seem so relaxed, so in control, and cool under pressure." On one occasion, a colleague told me, "Dude, if you were any more mellow, you'd be dead." I was very skilled at maintaining a calm and unflappable exterior, yet turmoil raged inside me.

My old school had a very strong math program, so by the end of fourth grade, I was already skilled at long division. My new school did not introduce long division until the fifth grade, so when I arrived, I was labeled "the smart kid." I was no slouch at my old school, but nobody ever called me the smart kid. I liked the new label, quickly identified with it, and began to put pressure on myself to perform academically.

I accepted nothing less than straight A's or a perfect score of one hundred percent on tests. A score of ninety percent or a B+ felt like a failure and sometimes brought me to tears. I couldn't stand the thought of missing a school day, as it might mean missing something important and falling behind. This extreme perfectionism had likely always been within me, but it had been reinforced and intensified by all the changes in my life.

I worked hard to maintain my identity as "the smart kid," and my efforts paid off. Eight years later, in 1982, I graduated as valedictorian of my high school class, which had over 200 students. I then went on to graduate Summa Cum Laude from engineering school in 1986.

The pressure I put on myself was intense. I developed some obsessive-compulsive behaviors, such as checking my homework and books dozens of times to ensure everything was in order before heading to class each day. One day, I lost my homework because I kept opening my notebook to confirm it was there. I was an extreme perfectionist about certain things but not about everything. For instance, I was never a neat freak; I didn't mind if my shirt was wrinkled, and I didn't care about organizing the socks in my drawers.

Being a perfectionist was generally an asset in school and engineering. However, it could at times become a liability because I often found it challenging to complete a project, constantly striving for improvement. Not surprisingly, many successful professionals exhibit perfectionist tendencies; however, as we will see later—*extreme perfectionism is often at the root of psychosomatic pain.*

During my college years, I experienced migraines two to three times a week and developed a TMJ disorder (Temporomandibular Joint Disorder) from grinding my teeth at night. This sometimes caused my jaw to lock in a painful spasm, particularly when I opened my mouth to eat breakfast first thing in the morning. The pain and cramping in and around my jaw and face were excruciating and quite frightening. My dentist explained that the constant tightness in my jaw, caused by grinding my teeth, was the source of the spasms, and that a clenched jaw is often related to stress. To alleviate the issues, I used a custom-fitted mouth guard while sleeping, which was helpful. Additionally, I established a routine of going to the gym after classes every day, benefiting both my TMJ disorder and the early stages of my migraines.

Around the same time, I began to experience dysphagia, which is difficulty swallowing. I had to be very careful to chew my food slowly and drink plenty of water; otherwise, it might become stuck in my esophagus, almost as if there were a blockage. This discomfort often triggered a panic reaction similar to choking, even though my breathing remained unaffected. If this occurred in public, I would quickly find a private place where I could jump up and down to dislodge the food.

Some of these swallowing incidents were frightening, so I eventually consulted my doctor about them. He was concerned that I might have a growth in my esophagus and recommended a test that involved drinking a special liquid while an X-ray technician observed it going down. No physical obstruction was found, which led the doctor to conclude that my symptoms were likely stress-related. He suggested trying meditation to help me relax. However, I had been taught in various churches throughout my life that meditation was an Eastern practice to be avoided, so I did not pursue his suggestion. The dysphagia, migraines, and TMJ disorder persisted for many years, and that was only the beginning of my struggles.

Chapter 2

STRANGE PAIN

Migraine and TMJ disorders are quite common, and it is generally understood that mental stress can trigger these conditions. However, the symptoms I experienced next were anything but typical. It was the fall of 1991, and I was engaged to be married. My fiancée and I had purchased a house together near my parents' home, and we were busy planning the wedding and the start of our new life together. I had a great job as an engineer, went to the gym daily, and was in good health. One day, while driving to work in my Toyota 4x4 truck, I hit a large bump in the road and felt a sharp pain deep inside my body. The truck had a stiff suspension, so I initially dismissed it as a cramp or a gas bubble jolted by the rough ride. A few days later, after hitting another big bump, I experienced a similar sensation, and this time, I paid closer attention.

The strange pain in my body grew increasingly intense over the next few months, and it wasn't just when I drove over bumps. It felt as though a foreign object was lodged inside me whenever I sat down. I was scared and convinced that I had a tumor or some other type of growth. My bowel movements became extremely painful, and I experienced odd sensations in my abdomen that felt like pins being stuck into me. Like many men, I was reluctant to see a doctor, but my fear ultimately drove me to schedule an appointment.

The doctor was uncertain about the cause of my pain but recommended that if it continued to worsen, I should get a CT scan. A few weeks later, both the pain and my anxiety had intensified, so I scheduled the test. By that point, I had not shared any of this with my fiancée or family members.

After the CT scan, I received a call from the hospital informing me that I needed to schedule an appointment to discuss the results with a specialist. They referred me to a local urologist. When I entered his office a week later, I was trembling inside, bracing myself for bad news. The urologist greeted me with a warm smile and invited me to take a seat.

He said, "I have your test results and would like to ask you a few questions. Have you changed jobs recently? Are you getting married or divorced? Are you moving? I found these questions strange coming from a urologist, and I was surprised by how much he seemed to know about my life. I confirmed that I was getting married in a few months, had just purchased my first home, and was getting ready to move out.

He nodded and said—"*It looks like you have a bad case of pain in the butt.*" My CT scan revealed that I had an inflamed prostate gland, a condition known as prostatitis. The doctor explained that it is often associated with major life events when seen in younger men. I sat there in disbelief as he continued, noting that he had encountered this before.

He prescribed a sedative and a smooth muscle relaxant, assuring me that I would feel better soon. As he showed me to the door, he asked me to call him in a week to update him on my condition.

After leaving the doctor's office, I sat in my truck for a few minutes, reflecting on what had just happened. I struggled to understand how such a thing was possible. I could see the connection between mental stress and migraines, but how could my prostate be affected by my thoughts? It didn't make sense to me, and I was skeptical. I wasn't feeling any nervousness or tension about the upcoming wedding or the house purchase, so the diagnosis didn't add up. It also seemed strange that my regular doctor wasn't aware of this phenomenon. However, I was deeply relieved that nothing serious was wrong with me. In the end, I decided not to fill the two prescriptions because I didn't feel I needed a sedative, and I was cautious about potential side effects.

I later learned that this phenomenon is not typically taught in medical schools, though many urologists are familiar with it. At that time, there was no internet to research such topics, and I was unaware of any books on psychosomatic pain, so I felt completely in the dark.

Driving to work the next morning, I noticed that I felt slightly better, and this improvement continued through the following day. By the third day, the pain that had troubled me for six months was completely gone, without any need for pills or treatments. As I drove over the same bumps in the road, I felt nothing but immense relief and freedom—it was truly amazing. The strange pin-like sensations in my abdomen had also disappeared.

The urologist did not perform any surgery, nor did I take the medications he prescribed. However, he gave me something I truly needed—*awareness* of the subtle, automatic, and unconscious thoughts related to significant life events that were affecting my body. These major life events often lead to anxious thoughts and feelings, but I had been suppressing them and remained unaware of their impact.

The pain never returned, and I learned a valuable lesson—anything you are *unaware* of can control you. My unconscious thoughts were causing real pain and creating inflammation that was visible on a CT scan. Awareness is powerful—in some cases, gaining new awareness is all that is needed for a cure.

After this experience, I tried sharing it with close friends and other doctors, but I was often met with polite smiles and puzzled expressions. The idea of a mind-body connection linked to major life events felt revolutionary—a concept that everyone should be aware of. However, I quickly learned to keep it to myself. After more than thirty years, I have come to trust the powerful truth of mind-body healing, and I'm encouraged by the growing body of testimonies and research that affirm its power.

Five years later, my wife and I were raising two healthy little boys, and everything was going well. That summer, in late August, we spent a long weekend at a family camp in the Adirondacks. With my oldest son starting school in about a week, this was our last outing of the summer.

Even though I did well in school and was seen as the smart kid, my unhappy experience of moving at the age of ten taught me to dread the end of summer and the start of a new school year. This fear was heightened by the fact that the beginning of school always meant suffering from severe migraine pain. Even as an adult—a heavy, dark feeling washed over me whenever back-to-school commercials aired on TV, making me feel unwell.

On this occasion, I stood by the lake with my young boys when someone walked by and casually remarked to my older son, "Labor Day is coming, then off to school—summer's over." Hearing those words triggered a wave of emotions, ranging from sadness to anger. It was a strange and overwhelming feeling that I couldn't shake for the rest of the weekend.

The next day, while my wife and the boys slept in, I set out on an early morning guided canoe trip along a beautiful stream winding through the boreal forest of the central Adirondacks. The paddling was challenging, as we had to navigate a strong current for several miles while heading upstream. The need for concentration distracted me from the dark mood I had experienced the day before, and I realized how silly it was to worry about the start of school when it had little to do with me. I returned to the camp later that morning feeling a bit better— though my elbows were curiously sore—and a lingering sense of dread still hovered over me.

We arrived home on Sunday evening, and the next morning, I woke up with both elbows feeling quite sore. I wondered if I had overdone it while paddling. As someone who owned two canoes and was an avid canoeist, I had made many long and challenging trips in the Allagash Wilderness of Maine, northern Minnesota, and Ontario's Quetico and Algonquin parks. I had never experienced any issues with my elbows.

The soreness persisted for several weeks, so I mentioned it to a friend who is an avid kayaker. "Oh yeah," he said, "I had that happen once on a weeklong kayak trip when I had to paddle hard over the shallows. It can take a long time to heal—maybe a few months. You need to take it easy for a while."

However, six months later, I still felt pain in both elbows whenever I needed to grip something. Reaching into the refrigerator for a carton of orange juice was excruciating. When I spoke to my doctor about the issue during my next regular physical, he said it was a common overuse injury. He advised me to rest and take anti-inflammatory medications like Ibuprofen.

Over the next few years, there were times when the pain would lessen, only to flare up again suddenly. A flare-up could be triggered by something as simple as picking up a bag of groceries incorrectly. Even when the pain had diminished, applying pressure to the bones inside or outside either elbow still caused discomfort. I repeatedly mentioned this to my doctor, but he provided no solutions.

The condition became chronic and persisted for the next twenty years, with no cure available except for rest and temporary relief from anti-inflammatory drugs. The pain was always present, fluctuating between slightly better and worse. I attributed its ongoing presence to my weightlifting and dirt biking, both of which I was unwilling to give up. Many people seemed to complain about tennis elbow, so I accepted it as normal.

I never forgot the day it all began on that innocent little paddle up the Adirondack stream, along with the dark feelings that overwhelmed me that same weekend. Despite having dealt with prostatitis in the past, it never occurred to me that my elbow issues could be connected to my thoughts or emotions. That idea seemed too far-fetched to consider. To this day, it remains difficult for me to fathom—and I find it awkward to write about. *However, there would come a day when the elbow pain would dramatically dissolve and never return.*

Around the same time my elbow troubles started, I began to feel pain in both my ankles every morning as soon as I got out of bed. When I talked to my doctor about it, he expressed concern because the pain affected both ankles instead of just one, as bilateral pain can sometimes suggest an inflammatory disease. However, he never mentioned that it could be related to my bilateral elbow pain. He advised me not to worry as long as the pain lasted no more than half an hour each day.

For the next twenty years, I hobbled around for about thirty minutes each morning to loosen up my ankles, and then I felt fine. If I sat for long periods, the pain would return, and I would limp around until it eased again. I convinced myself that the problem stemmed from regularly hitting my feet and ankles while riding my dirt bike on the rocky trails of New England.

In 1995, I made a career transition from a slow-paced military environment to a fast-paced commercial telecom setting. Shortly after starting my new position, I began experiencing discomfort in my neck. It started with occasional cramps but gradually worsened over a year or two until I was constantly aware of it. Some days, I struggled to turn my head to the left, while on others, I found it difficult to turn to the right. Although I felt significant stress from meeting tight deadlines and dealing with a demanding boss, I did not connect my neck pain to that stress. Many coworkers complained of stiff necks, which often came up in casual conversations, leading me to accept it as a normal side effect of a desk job and not associate it with any emotional factors. I bought a book with effective neck stretches and developed a morning routine that involved sitting on the floor and slowly turning my neck from left to right until it loosened up. This process took about twenty minutes, but it was beneficial. I followed that routine every single day for the next twenty years.

All of my physical symptoms—migraine, tendonitis, neck and ankle pain, TMJ, and dysphasia—were certainly bothersome, yet life was going relatively well during that time. However, I was unprepared for the challenges that lay ahead. A few years later, everything suddenly turned upside down, and life would never be the same again.

Chapter 3

LIFE TURNS UPSIDE DOWN

In the winter of 2001, following the birth of our third son, Ayden, our lives were turned upside down. I carried him from the hospital delivery room to the nursery, just as I had done with his two older brothers. However, when the pediatrician met me there this time, he pointed out several physical anomalies. Ayden had a transverse crease across both palms (a Simeon crease), webbed toes, undescended testicles, crooked fingers, and many other noticeable birth defects.

In the following months, various genetic tests were conducted, but they yielded no definitive answers. The geneticist we consulted informed us that something was wrong, but it could not be identified at that time. As genetic testing advanced in the subsequent years, more tests were carried out, yet we still found no answers.

Ayden experienced significant delays in reaching each milestone of physical and mental development and suffered from severe food allergies. For the first two years of his life, he could only consume a special prescription amino acid formula, which left him small and weak. As time passed, it became evident that he faced serious behavioral issues and intellectual disabilities. Our lives became a whirlwind of appointments with neurologists, urologists, gastroenterologists, geneticists, physical therapists, psychiatrists, behavioral therapists, and general practitioners.

Ayden struggled to regulate his emotions, which often led to violent outbursts directed at family members, pets, and sometimes even strangers in public. Our family lived in a constant state of fear and uncertainty about what he might do next. Despite these challenges, Ayden started kindergarten on time, although there were numerous incidents of aggression, impulsivity, and unpredictability. He remained in public school until the beginning of second grade, but despite our best efforts, he had to leave the public school system because of his aggressive behavior.

The first school Ayden attended was a private institution for children with intellectual and behavioral challenges, but the transition was difficult. Traditional methods like isolating him in a padded "time-out" room only worsened his behavior, leading to frequent physical restraints and growing distress for everyone. After three difficult years, we transferred him to a new school that adopted a more flexible and compassionate approach. Though the adjustment was rocky, Ayden eventually found his footing, made close friends, and remained there through graduation. I'm forever grateful to the staff who truly saw him and created a plan that helped him thrive.

One drawback of leaving the mainstream school system is that peers often have issues that are similar to or even worse than your own—rather than serving as positive role models. Ayden often came home displaying shocking new behaviors and language he had picked up from his classmates. He seemed to know every four-letter word, obscene expression, and inappropriate gesture imaginable. Each time he became emotionally dysregulated at home, we faced a new barrage of foul language and gestures.

He also learned many violent expressions and made frightening threats. Thankfully, he never actually attacked us, but he did cause significant damage to our home and inflict some injuries on our dogs. We never tolerated foul language or behavior in our home, but we felt powerless to stop these episodes of swearing and aggression when he was dysregulated. Ayden knew right from wrong, and after each incident, he would reset and apologize profusely. However, it was distressing to witness our two older boys regularly exposed to this language and behavior.

After Ayden was born, our relatively normal lives underwent a dramatic change. My wife and I stopped going on date nights. Instead, we began meeting with doctors and behaviorists, averaging twice a week, year after year, in our efforts to manage Ayden's health issues and violent behaviors. Consequently, my two older boys didn't receive the attention they deserved—*this troubled me greatly and ultimately resulted in even more pain.*

I had an extensive collection of books on child-rearing, and we met with several behaviorists, but mostly we received simplistic solutions that made us feel like incompetent parents. The only comfort was that our older boys were doing well despite the chaos at home.

One major issue we faced was Ayden's inability to sleep in his bed. Despite our best efforts, he would climb into our bed every night or lie on the floor beside us. I gently marched him back to his bed literally thousands of times over several years, but he never seemed to get it. When he turned six, we consulted a child psychiatrist who emphasized—"you must not lose this battle" and even suggested, somewhat dramatically, that we "use duct tape if necessary to keep him in his bed." I assumed he was exaggerating to make a point. The nightly bedtime struggles continued until Ayden was ten years old, when he finally managed to sleep through the night in his bed for the first time. Chronic sleep deprivation—which we will see is a catalyst for chronic physical pain—significantly affected all of us.

Eventually, we found an excellent psychiatrist who connected well with Ayden and understood his unique challenges. We have been meeting with him regularly for many years, refining strategies, adjusting medications, and continuing to do so as of this writing.

As Ayden entered puberty, his aggressive behavior increased. Our home displayed numerous dents and holes in the walls, along with a few broken windows from his outbursts. At times, he would storm out of the house in a rage and wander the neighborhood, refusing to return. My wife and I would chase after him, both on foot and by car, trying to coax him home without causing a scene in front of our neighbors.

Without a diagnosis, I convinced myself that I could fix all of Ayden's behavioral issues and teach him the academic skills necessary for future success and independence. He was highly motivated by social interactions and understood that reading was essential for accessing social media, including text messages and emails. Despite the challenges he faced, he learned to read with plenty of support.

However, Ayden struggled with math and had difficulty grasping basic concepts, such as counting, simple addition, and subtraction. Having volunteered as a math tutor for many years at an inner-city school, I took pride in my ability to teach math. I tried to teach Ayden the basics by placing numbers on the stairs in our house and counting as we walked up and down. We practiced this hundreds of times, and there were moments when he seemed to understand—yet the learning never stuck, and each day felt like starting over.

The same challenges arose when I attempted to modify his behaviors using positive and negative reinforcement. We had some success with point systems and rewards, which he seemed to grasp, but his impulsive behavior often sabotaged the process.

It took twenty years to secure a diagnosis because the proper tests were not available until recently. In 2021, at the age of twenty, Ayden was diagnosed with Chung-Jansen Syndrome, a spontaneous genetic mutation that is extremely rare. At the time of his diagnosis, only fifty known cases existed worldwide; by 2024, that number had grown to just four hundred. Chung-Jansen affects a gene responsible for synthesizing proteins in the brain and muscle tissue. While it was a relief to finally understand what was wrong, there is no cure for this condition. Fortunately, there are therapies and medications to address specific behavioral and emotional challenges. For more information about this syndrome, refer to Appendix B.

Around the time Ayden entered puberty and his behavior began to deteriorate, my mother was diagnosed with Lewy Body Dementia. This type of dementia resembles Alzheimer's disease but presents more physical symptoms that affect balance and walking. Her condition declined rapidly. My dad had passed away a few years earlier, and since Mom lived alone about ten minutes away, I was entrusted with her care, as my siblings did not live nearby.

I managed to keep her at home for the next four years by coordinating various levels of in-home support, but it was an extremely difficult situation. Finding aides willing to work overnight was challenging, and those who did often charged exorbitant rates, so we postponed overnight care for as long as possible. Mom was generally okay during the day, but at night, she sometimes became confused and would call the police, who then contacted me. Living in a small town, the police became familiar with our situation. Additionally, she occasionally wandered around the neighborhood, prompting neighbors to call me in the middle of the night to retrieve her. I don't believe I had a single night of uninterrupted sleep during those four years, but no one wanted to place her in a care home, so I did everything I could to manage the situation for as long as possible.

While my mom was deteriorating, my wife's aunt and uncle were also beginning to experience cognitive issues, and I was the only one available to assist them. They lived thirty minutes away, so I spent half of each Saturday shopping for them and taking care of their home and yard. I was glad to help, but I often felt rushed from one obligation to the next, struggling with exhaustion from a lack of sleep.

At the same time, my two older sons were starting college, and I was assisting them with their applications while figuring out how to finance their education. The financial pressures were overwhelming, and although I felt uneasy about taking out large loans, I had no choice but to do so. Despite these challenges, I believed I was managing well. I wasn't feeling especially anxious or depressed; I was addressing situations as they came up.

After my older sons went off to college, I took Ayden to our usual family camping spot in the Adirondacks near Lake George. Ayden loved camping and, as a young teenager, appreciated having my full attention. While we unpacked our gear at the campsite, I noticed three tin cups with the boys' names printed on them. A wave of sadness washed over me when I realized that my two older boys were not there. This feeling quickly grew into overwhelming sorrow as I looked at the empty cups on the table. I tried to shake it off—but no matter how hard I tried, I couldn't.

Throughout the weekend, those painful emotions replayed every time we visited a familiar spot—constantly reminding me of my older boys' absence. My sadness was worsened by the fact that, due to Ayden's overwhelming behavioral and health issues, the older boys often missed out. I felt guilty for not being able to give them the attention they deserved. By the end of the weekend, my sadness had turned into a heavy, dark mood. Although I put on a happy face for Ayden and tried to make the best of things, I was hurting deeply inside and felt close to tears.

We drove home on a Sunday night, and when I stepped out of the car, a sudden jolt of pain shot through my left hip. It hurt so much that I could barely walk into the house. On Monday morning, the pain persisted, and I was limping badly. Weeks passed, but the hip pain continued. I tried heat, massage, anti-inflammatory medications, and stretching—but nothing seemed to help. I racked my brain trying to remember what might have caused it, and assumed it must be related to our swimming in the lake by the campsite. I figured I had overstrained my hip joint and needed to give it time to heal. However, when I still had trouble walking months later, I consulted my doctor.

He performed a thorough examination but was unable to identify the issue. He suspected it might be a case of atrophying muscles around the hip. Despite my active lifestyle, which included plenty of walking and jogging, he suggested I incorporate an activity that requires lateral movement, such as basketball or tennis. I eventually found that I could achieve short-term relief by performing lateral leg lifts and maintaining a contracted hip flexor muscle for a few minutes at a time.

A few months later, I was dismayed to find that my other hip had begun to hurt in the same way. I convinced myself that I was in terrible physical shape, despite lifting weights and running on a treadmill five days a week. As a result, I added hip exercises targeting the painful areas to my daily workouts. Unfortunately, this provided only minimal relief, and the hip pain persisted.

Given my past experience with prostatitis and how I found healing through self-reflection and awareness, you might think I would have connected my new symptoms to the emotions I was experiencing—but I didn't. Busyness often gets in the way of awareness and can hide these connections. It's often said that busyness is a disease of our culture, acting as a form of suppression that is destructive to health and well-being, and I was a clear example of this. Despite the many challenges life threw at me, I truly believed I was coping well, but in hindsight, I was too busy to fully experience my anxiety, anger, or depression.

The onset of hip pain was only the tip of the iceberg. A few months later, new and worsening pain levels emerged that ultimately became debilitating.

Chapter 4

MY BACK IS ON FIRE

One December morning, several months after my camping trip with Ayden, I was rushing to get to work. It had been snowing lightly for a few hours, but the news reports indicated that it was raining in most areas. This was common since we lived at a relatively high elevation, so I often found myself as the only one arriving late to work, which bothered me. Determined not to be late for an important meeting, I grabbed a shovel and pushed myself to clear our long driveway as quickly as possible.

After forty minutes of frantic shoveling, I was finally done, but my lower back was on fire. This was nothing new—I often experienced back spasms, and they usually subsided within a few hours or, at worst, a few days. I hobbled to work feeling worse than ever, but I expected the pain to ease by the end of the day. Unfortunately, this time was different.

Days of pain turned into weeks, and weeks stretched into months. Some days were better than others, leading me to believe that I should wait it out instead of seeing a doctor. I found it hard to sleep because I had to keep changing positions to find relief. Mornings were the worst—getting out of bed became a slow and painful process, followed by carefully descending the stairs while facing backward. At work, I had to get up and move around every twenty minutes. Sometimes, the pain was so severe that it took my breath away, leaving me in tears and gasping for air. I kept delaying a visit to the doctor because I experienced short periods of partial relief that lasted a few days or sometimes a week or more, which made me believe I had turned a corner. However, the pain always returned with a vengeance.

I tried various methods to alleviate the pain. My wife and I invested in an expensive mattress tailored to our body types by a computerized machine. I read articles about the importance of good posture and made a conscious effort to sit correctly. I bought lumbar support devices and attached them to the chairs at home and work. I rearranged my desk, monitor, and keyboard to improve my ergonomics. I even purchased an inversion table and hung upside down daily for as long as I could tolerate it. Although hanging upside down caused blood to rush to my head and triggered severe headaches, I persevered for a few months. Ultimately, however, none of my physical efforts made any difference.

Gradually, after more than a year of pain, I began to notice alarming new symptoms. My lower back started to make grinding, crackling, and popping noises whenever I moved or twisted in specific ways. These sensations, along with the pain, frightened me—I worried that I might have a tumor, bone cancer, or some damage to my spine. By the spring of 2018, my anxiety had escalated to the point where I decided it was time to schedule an appointment with my doctor.

He ordered an X-ray of my lower back and hips to investigate the issue. The report was two pages long and detailed various problems with my spine. It revealed arthritis, osteophytes, stenosis, and bulging degenerated discs. The term "severe" appeared multiple times throughout the report. My doctor advised me not to be alarmed by the medical term "severe," explaining that many men over fifty have similar lower back issues—but mine were definitely worse than average. There was no specific explanation for my pain, and there were no signs of bone cancer or tumors, which was a relief.

A friend told me he heard that back pain can be psychosomatic and that there was a popular book about the subject. Given my history, this made sense, so I purchased the book and quickly skimmed through it. The book, titled *Healing Back Pain* by Dr. John Sarno, was endorsed by several well-known celebrities who claimed it had helped them. Dr. Sarno suggested that many cases of lower back pain stem from emotional stress, especially suppressed anger and anxiety, rather than structural issues in the back. Considering my previous experiences with migraines and prostatitis, I recognized that such connections could be possible. However, when I mentioned this book to my doctor, he dismissed the idea, urging me not to buy into that nonsense. Instead, he recommended that I see an orthopedist, who then ordered an MRI.

Like the X-ray report, the MRI report also listed numerous issues with my back. The orthopedist, similar to the previous doctor, noted that some of this was typical for someone my age. However, she confirmed that my back was much worse than average and suggested I might benefit from a series of steroid injections around the spine, as well as physical therapy. I couldn't help but ask if she believed psychological stress could be a factor, so I shared some of my history with her and the book I had read. She smiled politely and said it was very unlikely.

Due to the associated risks, I decided to postpone the injections and try physical therapy first. The following week, I met with the therapist and asked for his opinion on my MRI results. However, he informed me that he had not seen the MRI and had no details about my case other than the fact that I needed therapy for my lower back. The approach to lower back physical therapy seemed rather generic.

The therapy was based on a method that involves lying face down, similar to a push-up position, with the lower back arched upward and held in that position for as long as possible. Although this exercise was quite painful, the therapist assured me it would be beneficial. I did some research, and the method appeared to be supported by solid medical science. The therapist also recommended a book with additional exercises I could do at home to complement the bi-weekly therapy sessions. Excited about this approach, I diligently performed all the exercises and attended as many sessions as my insurance would cover—but I saw no improvement.

I asked the therapist if there could be a connection between my pain and mental stress, but, like the previous doctors I had consulted, he dismissed the idea, saying, "No way, you've got real pain going on here."

After more than two years of living with back pain, I began to experience new symptoms in other areas of my body. I had difficulty using my computer mouse while performing detailed CAD (Computer-Aided

Design) work at the office. CAD work requires precision for drawing schematics or laying out circuit boards, and my right hand would go numb after just fifteen minutes of using the mouse. A painful burning sensation in my forearm preceded the numbness. Everyone I spoke to, including my doctor, suggested that this was a repetitive stress injury (RSI). A coworker recommended switching to an ergonomic trackball instead of a mouse. I tried using the trackball, but it felt awkward and did not relieve the numbness.

The issue with the mouse became so severe that I had to teach myself to use it with my left hand. This was no simple task—it was like a baseball pitcher learning to throw with their non-dominant hand. It took months of practice, but I had no choice since I couldn't perform my job with my right hand. Gradually, I became proficient at using the mouse with my left hand.

However, over time, I began to feel the same burning and numbness in my left hand. To cope, I started alternating between my left and right hands every fifteen minutes throughout the day; more than a few of my colleagues noticed this strange behavior. I wondered how I could develop a repetitive stress injury (RSI) in my left hand, especially since I had only been using it for mousing for a few months. Once again, I feared that something was seriously wrong with me.

I did some research, and the pattern of numbness in my hands seemed to align with ulnar nerve compression at the elbow. I suspected that my chronic elbow tendonitis might have affected the nerves in both elbows, which was affecting my ability to use my hands. A colleague had undergone surgery for ulnar nerve compression because she was having trouble typing, so this made sense, and I planned to see a nerve specialist.

Aside from affecting my work, my symptoms also limited my ability to ride my motorcycle. I enjoyed riding to work when the weather was nice, but the problems with my hands made it dangerous. The right hand is essential for controlling the throttle and brake on a motorcycle, so maintaining good dexterity is crucial for safety. I found that I couldn't ride for more than fifteen minutes without feeling burning and numbness in both hands. Additionally, after just ten minutes in the saddle, the back of my neck felt as if it were on fire.

Desperate to keep riding, I tried several lightweight helmets to ease the strain on my neck, but they didn't help. I ordered special nerve-protecting gloves and throttle-assist devices to relax my hands and improve blood flow, but nothing worked. I even purchased an expensive after-market cruise control system for my street bike. This was effective on the open road, but I had to give up street riding after several near accidents in heavy traffic. In the end, I had to sell my street bike which I loved, a Triumph Tiger 800, and return to riding a dirt bike in the woods. Riding off-road eliminated the risk of cars and trucks, allowing me to pause every few minutes to rest my hands and neck.

Next, I faced difficulties while driving my car. I felt a burning sensation followed by numbness in my right foot, extending up the back of my leg to my buttocks. The only way I could keep steady pressure on the accelerator was by constantly adjusting my posture, and at times, I had to sit almost sideways in my seat. I used cruise control as much as possible, which wasn't practical in heavy traffic.

At that time, my middle son was attending school in Indiana and needed a car, so I bought a used Corolla to drive out to him. Unfortunately, this vehicle lacked cruise control, which was a major issue. I had to accelerate slightly above the speed limit, then ease off the gas pedal and coast until the feeling returned to my foot. I managed fine in the hills of Pennsylvania, where I could rest my foot while coasting downhill; however, the flat stretches of highway in the Midwest were grueling, often forcing me to pull over and stop. As a result, the drive took several hours longer than it should have. I was hesitant to see a doctor about these new symptoms because they hadn't helped with the others.

Three doctors had dismissed the idea that my pain was caused by mental stress, so I believed them and increasingly thought I had a serious but undiagnosed illness. I've never been one to complain about my personal problems, so I kept most of this to myself, which probably made things worse. I tried to avoid talking about my issues with my wife, children, and coworkers as much as possible. I bottled up the fear that something was seriously wrong, and it was really starting to haunt me.

One morning, while I was driving to work, I heard a radio advertisement looking for volunteers for a medical study on Ankylosing Spondylitis (AS). The ad mentioned that anyone experiencing lower back or joint pain that worsens in the morning might be a good candidate. This caught my attention, especially since I experienced pain in my ankles every morning, and my back pain was definitely more intense during that time as well. To learn more about AS, I subscribed to a podcast focused on the condition. I learned that AS is an autoimmune disease that can be difficult to diagnose, as there is no single definitive test for it. I took note that many AS patients experienced a flare-up of symptoms during emotional stress. I shared my concerns with my doctor, who ordered some blood tests to check for inflammation; however, all the results came back negative. He thought it was unlikely that I had AS, but I remained suspicious, which fueled my growing fear.

The situation with my body was becoming unmanageable, but fortunately, subtle clues began to emerge that revealed the true source of my pain. These clues had always been there, but pain can cloud perception and limit awareness. It was only by a stroke of grace that I was able to see beyond my suffering and understand the reality of the situation.

Chapter 5

TURNING THE CORNER

After more than two years of suffering, I began to notice patterns in my lower back pain. Every morning at five o'clock, I took our two golden retrievers outside to do their business. They were lively, full of energy, and completely indifferent to my suffering. After bringing them back into the garage and settling them down, I had to get on my hands and knees to clean the mud off their eight paws before letting them back into the house. The pain I felt during this morning ritual was extreme and became a reference point for judging whether I was getting better or worse. *I realized that on the rare nights I enjoyed deep, uninterrupted sleep, I noticed a significant decrease in pain the following morning.* This pattern was both consistent and predictable—getting eight hours of deep, uninterrupted sleep made a noticeable difference in my pain level.

This observation, which took two years to sink in, opened me to the possibility that, despite my doctors' dismissive attitude, there was a connection between stress and tension similar to what I've always experienced with migraine. Anyone with migraine will tell you that if you can get a good night's sleep, the pain will most likely improve by the next morning. Unfortunately, I rarely got a good night's sleep due to my severe back pain, my son Ayden's behaviors, and my mom getting confused and calling me in the middle of the night.

A second pattern began to emerge during Saturday morning trips to the supermarket. I always took Ayden with me to give my wife a break, as he had a knack for pushing her buttons, and I felt that providing them with some time apart was essential. However, these trips consistently triggered severe flare-ups of my back pain, which at times were so intense that I could barely finish shopping. This was puzzling because pushing a shopping cart seemed like a very benign activity. I wondered if leaning slightly forward on the cart with my arms out-stretched was putting pressure on the nerves in my spine. So, for a few weeks, I tried pushing the cart with one hand while keeping myself perfectly upright to see if that made a difference. It was challenging to navigate corners with one hand on a fully loaded shopping cart, and it likely looked very peculiar, but after several weeks, it became clear that it made no difference.

I found the connection between back pain flare-ups and grocery shopping quite intriguing. Upon reflection, I realized it might be related to my son. Although Ayden was a teenager at the time, his intellectual abilities and emotional regulation skills resembled those of a five-year-old. As a result, managing him in the supermarket was quite challenging.

Despite his disabilities and challenging behaviors, Ayden was sociable, outgoing, and sought attention. He found great joy in identifying issues in the store and reporting them to a manager. One of his favorite games was to sneak away from me, locate a store manager, and declare that he had lost his father. To my dismay and Ayden's delight, the store manager would announce my name over the loudspeaker, "Would James Garrett please come to the courtesy booth? Your son is looking for you."

I don't like drawing attention to myself, so hearing my name broadcast over the loudspeaker almost every Saturday was humiliating. It announced to the entire store that I couldn't control my child—which upset me. I was convinced that everyone in town saw me as a delinquent parent, and I often left the store feeling humiliated, angry, and frustrated with my son. After a while, I began to think that this ongoing humiliation might be triggering my flare-ups. It made sense to me because I knew that if I went shopping with a migraine, such an event would definitely make it worse.

Another clue indicating a mind-body connection was that as my back pain worsened, I developed an unhealthy obsession with motorcycles—thinking about them constantly. I would sit and watch monotonous racing videos for hours and hours. I was always searching online for items to enhance my dirt bike's performance. I would go riding whenever possible, even if it meant waking up at 4 am and returning before everyone else woke up. I noticed similar obsessive behavior in others I knew who were struggling with personal issues, and I was now recognizing it within myself. I realized this was unhealthy and understood that I was suppressing negative thoughts, attempting to replace them with positive thoughts and activities. From my experience, I knew that suppressed thoughts and feelings could lead to trouble, which helped convince me to pursue a mind-body connection to my pain.

The final motivation I needed came from a memory of my father, who passed away years before my back pain began. When my dad turned fifty, he developed chronic lower back pain and, for two decades, regularly visited a chiropractor for relief. His pain persisted into his early seventies when he retired, and then, surprisingly, it disappeared. I remember asking him how his back felt, and he would say it was fine, even well into his eighties. At that stage of his life, my dad had poor posture and never exercised, yet he experienced no back pain. Looking back, the only factor I could associate with the resolution of his pain was his retirement from a stressful management job in the high-tech industry. After contemplating this, I realized I needed to explore what was going on in my mind.

I read Dr. John Sarno's book *The Mindbody Prescription*, which is a sequel to *Healing Back Pain*. In this book, he explains that physical symptoms, such as back pain, can serve as distractions—keeping our attention focused on physical pain and thus avoiding the need to consciously deal with unpleasant thoughts and feelings.[4] Based on my own experiences with migraines and prostatitis, this perspective resonated with me. However, I was skeptical about some of his broader claims. The book didn't focus on specific exercises or practices, so I didn't consciously make any changes to my life. The main idea was that once you recognize the psychological origins of pain and stop fearing a structural cause, the symptoms should diminish or disappear.

---

4. Sarno, The Mindbody Prescription, p 18

Dr. Sarno mentioned that many of his patients were perfection-ists—hardworking, conscientious, and driven professionals. I fit that personality profile, which encouraged me. However, he also indicated that some patients required psychotherapy because their emotional issues were quite deep, which concerned me.

Two weeks after reading *The Mindbody Prescription* twice, my lower back pain had not improved and may have worsened. According to the testimonies of others who have read the book, I should have started to feel better by then. Consequently, I concluded that I might be among those who needed psychotherapy. However, due to the stigma I asso-ciated with it, I was reluctant to explore that option. I began to feel discouraged about the entire mind-body connection and once again questioned whether something was seriously wrong with my back. I couldn't help but dwell on all the issues mentioned in my X-Ray and MRI results, and fear that I might have Ankylosing Spondylitis.

A few days after rereading *The Mindbody Prescription*, I found myself in my basement gym doing bicep curls and triceps extensions—exercises I didn't particularly enjoy because my elbows always hurt to some degree. However, I had learned to push through the discomfort, which had become normal for me after almost twenty years.

This time, though, something was different—*there was no pain*. I pressed on the bones on the inside and outside of each elbow where I usually felt discomfort, and to my surprise, there was none. I hadn't taken any anti-inflammatories in quite a while, and even when I did, I still experienced *some* pain. But that day, for the first time, my elbows were completely pain-free. I was pleasantly mystified.

Weeks passed, and I continued to work out without experiencing any pain in my elbows. Feeling confident, I began to do things I had previously learned to avoid. I reached into the back of the refrigerator and squeezed a carton of orange juice, an action that had always caused sharp pain in the past. To my surprise, there was no discomfort. I could squeeze or grip anything as tightly as I wanted from any angle, lift fur-niture with either hand, and still feel no pain. My elbow tendonitis had suddenly vanished and has not returned to this day.

This was completely unexpected, but I vaguely recalled something Dr. Sarno had mentioned about how tendons in different parts of the body could be affected similarly to the lower back. I searched through both of his books, and, sure enough, I found relevant information. In his practice, he observed that many patients also experienced a disappearance of tendon pain, such as tennis elbow, in addition to resolving their back pain.[5] I didn't fit the model he described, as my back still hurt worse than ever, but my elbows were suddenly fine.

The experience with my elbows was puzzling—but it gave me something to hang my hat on. I had simply read a book about the connection between the mind and lower back pain and half-believed its ideas. *I hadn't changed my mindset or adopted any new practices, so I concluded that the book had increased my awareness, which in turn affected some of my symptoms.* Although it seemed strange that the mind could cause tendonitis in the elbows, I couldn't deny what had happened. This concept was a significant intellectual stretch for me, and it still is today—so I rarely discuss it with anyone. Even among doctors who acknowledge the mind-body connection, joint tendonitis is typically not included in the list of common mind-body symptoms. Nevertheless, I feel compelled to share my experience here in the hope that it might help someone else.

After my unusual experience with my elbows, I bought every book I could find about the mind-body connection, especially those that included personal stories. I also watched numerous YouTube videos on the subject and subscribed to several podcasts. While these sources did not offer a clear, systematic therapy, the common theme was that releasing inner rage could lead to relief from pain.

While browsing mind-body topics on YouTube one day, I stumbled upon a soft-spoken man sitting on a stage in front of a small audience. The audience asked questions, and the man responded slowly, addressing each one individually. Someone asked a personal question that I can no longer recall, but I distinctly remember the man replying with

---

5. Sarno, Healing Back Pain, p 67

two simple words—"*Stop thinking.*" Those two words resonated with me and led me down a path that would change my life.

Chapter 6

STOP THINKING

The man who said to stop thinking was Eckhart Tolle. He was not a mind-body practitioner but rather a spiritual teacher who emphasized keeping your attention on the present to quiet the mind, which often dwells on the past and the future. He was not the kind of spiritual teacher I was used to, yet I recognized that my mind was always racing at a hundred miles per hour, so I thought I could learn something from him. I had never heard a sermon in church about how to quiet the mind. Additionally, I had volunteered as a Sunday school teacher for many years and had never seen this addressed in any standard curriculum, making the subject new to me. I had some experience quieting my mind while trying to fall asleep, but that was the extent of it.

I read Tolle's book, *The Power of Now* and its sequel, *A New Earth*, but neither book made sense to me. Tolle presented several concepts that I found strange, such as the idea that we are not our thoughts,[6] and he spoke about a body of old emotional and psychological pain that we carry inside.[7] I had a hard time accepting the idea of not being my thoughts, especially since my engineering background instilled a high regard for rational thinking.

At that time, I was wary of the practice of meditation, which Tolle frequently discussed. If you are one of the millions raised in the Western church, you've likely been taught to avoid meditation because it's considered "dangerous" and "Eastern." I remember walking into church as a kid in the mid-1970s and being handed a pamphlet warning about the dangers of meditation. It contained stern warnings about how the

---

6. Tolle, The Power of Now, p 11
7. Ibid., p 36

devil can exploit an empty mind, leaving a lasting impression on a nervous twelve-year-old. Many denominations teach that meditation leads to a dangerous, trance-like state that should be avoided. *While these warnings may seem absurd to those raised outside the church, the fear and stigma are very real for many.*

I used to believe that the Judeo-Christian scriptures did not encourage quieting the mind, but I later realized that this idea is implied throughout the texts. The scriptures admonish us to let go of thoughts related to worry, fear, anger, hatred, lust, unforgiveness, materialism, judgment, and the past. Since most repetitive and negative thoughts revolve around these issues, releasing them naturally leads to a very quiet mind. The truth is that freeing oneself from these vices can be difficult if one doesn't know how to quiet the mind.

I eventually learned that meditation is simply about gently taking control of your thoughts and emotions, instead of allowing your automatic programming to dictate them. I emphasize "gently" because it should not be a battle. Ultimately, I discovered that a quiet mind provides freedom from the world, freedom from past pain, and freedom from future worries. Why would anyone be against that?

In the preface to this book, I mentioned a mental game I learned as a child that helped me fall asleep at night and how my awareness of what was happening in this game opened me up to the concepts in Eckhart Tolle's books. I listened to his audiobooks repeatedly in my car for several months—probably ten times each. They taught me the importance of inner body awareness, which involves paying attention to the inner body and being aware of what is happening inside. Tolle explained that few people take the time to look inward and suggested that we periodically ask ourselves, "What's going on inside me now?"[8] This practice resonated with me, and I found it quite satisfying.

I quickly discovered that there was always something happening within me. Whenever I tried to sit quietly, my mind would fill with mental chatter. Some of this chatter was useful and constructive,

8. Tolle, The Power of Now, p 27

especially when I was addressing a technical problem at work, but most of it was just noise. Although there were moments of clarity, calmness, and peace, they were fleeting. I realized this was not ideal and was likely connected to my physical pain. However, I struggled with meditation because my back hurt intensely, making it challenging to sit still and not tense up and fight the pain.

Regularly asking myself, "What's going on inside me now?" didn't alleviate my pain, but it did help me become more aware. I noticed a subtle emotional tension, or knot, in my gut that was always present, distinct from the intense pain in my lower back. This feeling resembled the occasional anxiety or distress that one might experience, but it lingered at a low level and never entirely disappeared. Each time I sat quietly and turned inward, I became aware of this persistent sensation in my gut.

I read several other books in the same genre, including *The Untethered Soul* by Michael Singer, an accomplished software developer and businessman with whom I immediately identified. When I first read *The Untethered Soul*, I didn't fully understand it, but I found myself returning to it again and again. I also read his second book, *The Surrender Experiment*, which was quite different and captivated my attention. Singer's teachings on surrender resonated deeply with me, echoing the idea of embracing the sovereignty of the Divine—a principle I had been taught in churches throughout my life. Months later, as I revisited the concept of surrender, I experienced a profound breakthrough, which I will discuss in the next chapter.

Michael Singer emphasized the importance of relaxing into unpleasant emotions instead of fighting or pushing them away. He taught that negative emotions are stored deep within us, much like the concept of a body of old emotional and psychological pain. As we navigate life, past emotional energy can be triggered, seeking acknowledgment and release. The problem arises when we resist this energy instead of allowing it to flow through us. His technique for finding freedom is straightforward—whenever you notice an emotional disturbance, relax and allow the energy to release.[9] He also teaches that when you think you've relaxed enough, you should relax even more. I started practicing this, but it was challenging at first. My mind would attach stories to my negative emotions, creating tension instead of relaxation. I continued to practice relaxation with small things daily, and after a few months, I gradually started to grasp the concept.

The next book I came across was *Back in Control* by Dr. David Hanscom. Dr. Hanscom is a renowned spine surgeon who, based on his own experiences, discovered that many cases of lower back pain can be resolved through emotional counseling instead of surgery. He employs a multifaceted approach called the DOC (Direct your Own Care) program.[10]

Dr. Hanscom's foundational practice for all his patients is expressive writing, which I had already heard about on several mind-body podcasts. This involves sitting in a chair once or twice a day for 15 minutes to write down any thoughts that come to mind. It is important to use pen and paper, disregarding spelling, grammar, punctuation, and neatness. During this time, you express your most private and uncomfortable thoughts. Once you have finished writing, you tear the paper into small pieces and throw them away.

Using a computer for this exercise is not advisable because the document can be saved and potentially viewed by others. Furthermore, typing does not engage the brain in the same way that writing by hand does. The aim is to write freely without the fear of others seeing your thoughts. Both positive and negative thoughts should be written down as they come up.

Although I had come across the concept of expressive writing before, I was hesitant to try it. The idea never appealed to me—it seemed like a feminine activity, akin to keeping a diary or journal, which many men tend to shy away from. Overall, it felt awkward and uncomfortable, and I saw it as a waste of time. However, Dr. Hanscom,

---

9. Singer, The Untethered Soul, p 105
10. Hanscom, Back in Control, p 4

a respected mind-body practitioner and spine surgeon, noted that *very few patients could bypass this step and become pain-free.*[11]

After reading his book twice, I finally decided to give it a try. One morning, I picked up a pen and paper and started writing. At first, it felt like a pointless exercise. On my first day, I wrote, "I don't feel like writing; this is a stupid waste of time." I began jotting down all kinds of random thoughts like that every day. If a happy thought crossed my mind, I would write it down along with my other musings. I recorded whatever chatter echoed in my head, only to tear it up and shred it afterward. Some of my thoughts were so embarrassing that I immediately erased or crossed them out—fearing someone might see them.

After a few weeks of writing down my thoughts twice a day, I noticed a change in my pain one morning as I got out of bed. The dogs were eagerly waiting to go outside, so I began my slow-motion ritual of sliding out of bed onto all fours and gradually pulling myself into an upright position. As I hobbled to the bathroom, I realized it didn't hurt as much this time.

With each passing day, I noticed a gradual improvement, and after a few more weeks of consistent writing, my back pain had improved by at least 50 percent. I was ecstatic to have finally discovered something that worked. As the weeks progressed, I continued to experience less and less back pain.

As I wrote down my thoughts each day, it became clear that I was harboring suppressed anger, even toward the people I loved most. I was angry about the difficulties caused by Ayden's violent behavior, which had disrupted our family. I was frustrated that I couldn't give my two older boys the attention they deserved, and that my marriage had suffered. I was angry with my mom, whose dementia had turned my life into a chaotic mess. I felt resentment towards my siblings who lived far away and couldn't help with my mom's care, and I was upset that they didn't fully understand the challenges I faced. I was also angry about the additional burden of caring for my wife's relatives, who were

---

11. Hanscom, Back in Control, p 191

struggling, with no one stepping in to assist. I felt angry *and scared* that no one could fix my painful back and that new symptoms kept emerging. I was frustrated that I could barely operate a computer mouse and struggled to do my job. I was upset that I couldn't ride a street bike and that I had difficulty driving a car.

Anger is prevalent in people with chronic pain,[12] and all mind-body practitioners have a lot to say about anger. When someone becomes stuck in chronic pain, it's often their anger that lies at the root of the problem, especially when they're unaware of it, as I was. The pain might not have started with anger, but chronic pain tends to breed anger because no one understands what you're going through—including doctors—which is hugely frustrating. Recognizing that I was suppressing a lot of anger encouraged me to write down my angry thoughts and feelings every day, which gradually helped reduce my pain.

I prefer the term "expressive scribbling" over "expressive writing" because it emphasizes jotting down thoughts without worrying about form, grammar, punctuation, spelling, neatness, or content. I often use shorthand or symbols to convey my thoughts and feelings. Instead of pondering what to write, I scribble out my thoughts and feelings as they come to me with complete abandon and no self-censorship.

I've found that writing twice a day is the most effective approach. In the morning, your thoughts can differ significantly from those in the evening. By writing at both times, you gain a better understanding of what's happening in your mind. Writing just before bed is particularly helpful—it allows your thoughts to settle, making it easier to fall asleep.

Numerous studies demonstrate the effectiveness of expressive writing in addressing anxiety and depression while also enhancing physical health. This technique is not new; it has been practiced for centuries in various forms. Expressive writing is often incorporated into cognitive behavioral therapy (CBT) for anxiety and depression, and research

---

12. https://pmc.ncbi.nlm.nih.gov/articles/PMC7578761 PMID: 32562660 retrieved 7/25/25

suggests that CBT can be as effective, if not more so, than other types of psychological treatments or even antidepressant medications.[13] More information about CBT can be found in Appendix A.

Why does expressive writing help alleviate chronic physical pain? Chronic pain is defined as pain that lasts for more than three to six months. When someone experiences pain for this long, their nervous system becomes overly active. Research shows that the human nervous system can amplify pain signals and even retain a memory of those signals.[14] Moreover, repetitive negative thoughts (RNTs) have been shown to have a detrimental effect on the nervous system.[15] Expressive writing helps to calm the nervous system and alleviate chronic pain by quieting RNTs.

The nervous system can remember and amplify real pain signals for months or even years after an injury has healed. A clear example of this phenomenon is "phantom limb pain," where amputees report feeling pain in pre-amputation lesions—*in a limb that is no longer there.* The amputees who experience this emphasize that they are suffering real pain, which they can describe in vivid detail, and insist that the experience is not imagined.[16] My own experiences with pain in my lower back and elbows began as injuries from shoveling snow and paddling a canoe, which likely healed within a few months. However, my nervous system memorized and amplified this pain for years afterward. It's important to note that this memorized pain is not imaginary—*it is very real and is perceived in the same way as the original injury.* Later, we will explore how RNTs can trigger chronic pain even in the absence of an injury, as I have experienced with conditions such as prostatitis, hip pain, and migraines.

Dr. Hanscom calls expressive writing "mechanical meditation" because it produces effects similar to traditional meditation, such as growing awareness and helping you separate from your thoughts and

13. https://pubmed.ncbi.nlm.nih.gov/32904947/ PMC7464866 retrieved 5/23/25
14. https://pmc.ncbi.nlm.nih.gov/articles/PMC4664460/ PMID: 25744681 retrieved 5/23/25
15. https://pmc.ncbi.nlm.nih.gov/articles/PMC9356323/ PMID: 35942479 retrieved 5/23/25
16. https://pubmed.ncbi.nlm.nih.gov/2293143/ PMID: 2293143 retrieved 5/23/25

feelings. However, expressive writing is much easier to practice when experiencing intense physical pain.

Expressive writing creates a separation between your eyes and the words on the paper, and between your hands and the words you write. The final act of tearing up, shredding, and discarding the paper helps bring about a more complete separation. As a result, you start to observe your thoughts and emotions instead of identifying with them—leading to a quieter internal space and greater awareness.

Awareness is your connection to reality, while thoughts and feelings can often be misleading. Repetitive negative thoughts are not only unhelpful—they can also be harmful. Anything that remains outside your awareness can control you, whereas anything within your awareness can be managed and controlled. Expressive writing helps bring thoughts that lie beneath the level of consciousness into full awareness.

If you are experiencing physical or emotional pain and do nothing else recommended in this book, I implore you to spend fifteen minutes twice a day jotting down your thoughts and feelings. If you are in extreme pain and cannot engage in traditional meditation, this is the way to do it. If you have religious objections to traditional meditation, expressive writing will achieve the same benefits. If your mind races like a herd of wild horses and you can't slow it down, this is the way to gently take control. If you are looking for a single pill to free you from emotional and physical pain without side effects, this is the closest thing you will find.

If you are experiencing chronic physical pain, I cannot emphasize enough the importance of getting a good night's sleep. Engaging in expressive writing just before bedtime can help calm your mind and make it easier to fall asleep. However, if you are still struggling with sleep, you should schedule an appointment with your doctor to explore solutions. If your doctor is unhelpful, consider seeking assistance from another physician. There is no shame in temporarily taking sleep medication to overcome this challenge.

I am not a sleep expert, but I am knowledgeable about electromagnetic fields. Studies have shown that sleep is influenced by the electromagnetic fields emitted by mobile phones, particularly when they are placed near the head, such as on a nightstand.[17] Keeping a phone nearby, even with the screen off, can produce a measurable change in the electrical activity in your brain, as indicated by an EEG, which can impact your ability to enter deep sleep. It is best to maintain a distance of at least four feet from your head, put your phone in airplane mode, or turn it off entirely while trying to sleep. It's also important to stay away from your phone for 30 minutes before bedtime. Before I understood this, I would place my phone next to my head while using the alarm app to wake up in the morning, and I would check messages and emails right before going to bed. Consequently, on nights when I needed sleep the most, I would often lie awake, puzzled about why I couldn't fall asleep. Removing the phone from the bedroom was the solution.

At this point in my journey, I had made significant progress and was on the path to healing, but something essential was still missing—*that missing element was surrender*. Surrender has the power to not only separate you from negative thoughts and feelings, but it also takes you deeper, where they are quelled, ensuring they can no longer trouble you. Although surrender is challenging to define concisely, we will explore it further in the next chapter.

17. https://pmc.ncbi.nlm.nih.gov/articles/PMC7320888/ PMID: 32607035 retrieved 5/23/25

Chapter 7

THE BREAKTHROUGH

One day, while listening to a talk by Michael Singer, a light bulb went on inside me. He explained the concept of surrender and emphasized the importance of letting go of future outcomes. He suggested that our focus should be on serving in the present and being okay with whatever happens in the future. Although I had heard this idea before, I initially dismissed it because I was always intensely focused on achieving specific goals and pursuing them with grim determination. At that moment, however, I realized that life rarely goes as we want or expect, and that fixating on specific goals often causes us to miss the bigger picture that we might not always see. Surrendering means accepting reality instead of fighting it and demanding that things happen a certain way. I saw that my struggle with life's realities was a major source of my anxiety and anger.

Raising a teenager with intellectual disabilities and severe behavioral issues can create significant anxieties about potential adverse outcomes. One of my main concerns was ensuring that my son could live independently and lead a productive life. I was determined to address all of his negative behaviors and envisioned him eventually "leaving the nest," just like his two older brothers. Although there are many opportunities for adults with special needs to live independently or in a group setting, a history of aggressive behaviors limits these options. The thought of him living with my wife and me for the rest of our lives was unacceptable, but it was starting to seem like a likely outcome.

I realized that I needed to stop resisting this possibility and be open to whatever the future might hold. Accepting this did not mean I was giving up—it meant giving Ayden my best effort without insisting that his future unfold as I envisioned. Once I accepted and surrendered to the reality of our situation—despite all the chaos in our lives—I found a new sense of peace and freedom.

To understand the concept of surrendering to outcomes, consider the difference between watching a sports game on TV with your favorite team and observing a match between two teams you don't know. When your favorite team plays, you care deeply about the outcome, causing your emotions to fluctuate as the game unfolds. If the game is close, you might feel nervous, yell, or even throw things at the TV. If your team wins, you feel ecstatic; if they lose, you feel depressed. Conversely, when you watch two unfamiliar teams without emotional attachment, you can relax and enjoy the game no matter who wins or loses.

When you have no specific preference for a particular outcome, life becomes an adventure, and every moment is embraced and enjoyed, even the challenging ones. You find joy in both winning and losing. You engage in every situation enthusiastically and give your best effort, then allow the outcome to unfold naturally. *While you still set goals, you no longer tie your identity to them—so they cannot affect your well-being.* By releasing your preferences, your mind and emotions settle into a quiet state—with nothing left for them to say.

Understanding surrender as letting go of outcomes was a breakthrough for me, and it ultimately led to the resolution of most of my physical pain. Physical pain is a severe reaction to long-term emotional stress, and a small shift in thinking was all it took for it to begin resolving. The physical pain disappeared relatively quickly, but it took much longer to release all the anxiety and anger. A deeper freedom from this emotional pain emerged through the long-term practice of surrender and the other stillness practices that you will learn about later in this book.

It took about six months for my back pain to mostly resolve, and during that time, I was so focused on my back issues that I hardly noticed when my neck pain completely disappeared. I hadn't expected relief from my neck pain, because I thought it was a normal consequence of having a desk job. Once I realized it was gone, I stopped doing the morning neck stretches I had practiced for twenty years.

Several months after my neck pain resolved, normal sensation returned to both hands. I hadn't anticipated this outcome because I was convinced I had a repetitive stress injury (RSI), particularly in my right hand. However, when I used my right hand again to operate the computer mouse, I felt no burning or numbness.

Gradually, normal sensation returned to my feet, the hip pain disappeared, and even my TMJ symptoms vanished. I found that I could drive long distances without using cruise control and ride my dirt bike without needing to stop to manage the numbness in my hands or rest my sore neck. The stress-induced migraines also subsided, although I remain careful to avoid specific food triggers and intense outdoor activities in extreme heat.

The morning ankle pain and difficulty swallowing lasted for more than a year, but those issues eventually went away, even though I wasn't expecting that.

One surprising outcome was that after my back pain resolved, the pain from an old shoulder injury disappeared. I had injured my left shoulder in high school and had lived with a torn rotator cuff for over thirty years. Imaging tests revealed a tear in one of the four tendons in my shoulder, which often bothered me, especially when lifting weights. Although I had the opportunity to have it surgically repaired many years ago, I opted against it because I didn't want to take five months off from my favorite activities for recovery. My left shoulder now feels just like my right shoulder.

This supports the idea that repetitive negative thoughts can over-stimulate the nervous system, amplifying pain signals that would otherwise be minor. By calming these thoughts, the nervous system also calms down, which can help reduce all types of pain, including that caused by physical injuries. Although my torn rotator cuff has not healed, the pain signals it sends are no longer amplified, making the discomfort barely noticeable.

I love cats, but I have always been allergic to them. However, once my pain resolved, my allergies changed as well. In the past, I had to limit my time at the homes of friends or family who had cats to avoid experiencing prolonged allergic reactions. After my pain subsided,

I noticed that I could stay in homes with cats for extended periods without significant reactions, experiencing only a minor response. This phenomenon is not uncommon; many people have found relief from various allergies once their minds and nervous systems have calmed down.

Months after my pain first began to subside, I had a strange experience I will never forget. I was driving on unfamiliar roads in another state, following the navigation app on my phone. At one point, traffic came to a standstill, so the app guided me down an alternate route through some sketchy neighborhoods where questionable characters were hanging around. I started to feel uneasy and noticed a swirl of negative thoughts and emotions. *Strangely, it felt like those thoughts and feelings belonged to someone else, and I was observing them from a distance.* I felt relatively relaxed and comfortable, yet I was aware of fear, agitation, and judgment, as if they were part of someone else's experience, and I didn't mind those emotions.

This was the first time I experienced anything like that, but afterward, similar experiences began happening regularly. I was starting to separate from, or disidentify with, negative thoughts and emotions. I gradually realized these negative feelings were not truly me—they represented a false self that was pretending to be me. This shift in perception resulted from expressive writing (mechanical meditation), learning to surrender, and the other stillness practices we will cover later.

Over time, it became normal for me to separate from my thoughts and feelings, a practice often referred to as being the "silent witness" or the "silent observer." I still experience anxiety, anger, and occasional depression; however, distancing myself from these emotions allows their energy to flow and dissipate quickly. Disturbances that once bothered me for hours now typically last only seconds or minutes before fading away. When they do linger, I can observe them from a distance, preventing them from significantly affecting me. In the upcoming chapters, we will go deeper into becoming a "silent observer."

It has been said that observing the inner body through meditation can slow down the aging process. When I first heard this idea, I thought it sounded silly; however, I have come to realize that it is true.

I now feel as I did thirty years ago, with little pain or tension in my body. I used to spend time each morning stretching my stiff body, but I no longer stretch, nor do I feel the need to.

My experience in this area is supported by scientific research. Chronic stress is known to accelerate aging by increasing cortisol levels. Meditation has been shown to significantly reduce cortisol levels.[18] Telomeres, which are the protective caps at the end of chromosomes, typically shorten with age. Some studies suggest that meditation may help maintain telomere length.[19] Additionally, chronic inflammation and oxidative stress are factors that contribute to the aging process, and meditation has been linked to reduced inflammation[20] and lower levels of oxidative stress.[21]

I also find that I get sick less often, and research supports the idea that meditation can bolster the immune system.[22] Whenever I feel a cold or flu coming on, I take time to relax and focus on my inner body, which helps me recover quickly. I will discuss how to respond to illness and fatigue in more detail in Chapter 22.

Many spiritual teachings emphasize the present moment, but for a long time, this idea felt abstract to me, and I couldn't grasp it. However, it has taken on new significance in my life. Nowadays, when I take a simple walk outdoors, I can quiet my mind and truly notice everything around me—every sound, every gentle breeze, the rhythm of my footsteps, the beauty of the sky, and the vibrant life surrounding me. In the past, such a walk would have triggered a flurry of labels, judgments, likes, dislikes, and a stream of thoughts about the past and future. It's difficult to convey the richness of this experience in words, so I invite you to learn how to quiet your mind and experience the present moment for yourself.

During the darkest part of my journey through pain, my mind was in constant overdrive. Many believe that nonstop thinking is unavoidable

---

18. https://pmc.ncbi.nlm.nih.gov/articles/PMC8763207/ PMID: 35046747 retrieved 7/14/25
19. https://pubmed.ncbi.nlm.nih.gov/31903785/ PMID: 31903785 retrieved 7/14/25
20. https://pmc.ncbi.nlm.nih.gov/articles/PMC4851883/ PMID: 26970711 retrieved 7/14/25
21. https://pubmed.ncbi.nlm.nih.gov/21280542/ PMID: 21280542 retrieved 7/14/25
22. https://pmc.ncbi.nlm.nih.gov/articles/PMC4940234/ PMID: 26799456 retrieved 7/14/25

or that it increases productivity, and I once shared that view. However, I've come to realize that incessant thinking is counterproductive and can even be harmful. As we'll see next, this never-ending mental activity can drain our energy, create tension, block creativity, and ultimately lead to both physical and emotional pain.

Chapter 8

INCESSANT THINKING

You don't need to be thinking every waking moment. Many of the thoughts you have today are the same ones from yesterday, and they haven't added anything useful. The mind can be like a hamster on a running wheel—busy but going nowhere. Unbeknownst to you, these repetitive thoughts drain your energy, causing fatigue and tension in your body. If you could replace these thoughts with periods of mental stillness, you would accomplish more with less energy drain and stress. A quiet mind will be sharp, focused, and ready for action when needed for something productive. Incessant and compulsive thinking is a tough habit to break—but learning to be mentally still is essential for your physical, mental, and spiritual well-being.

The mind naturally wants to stay busy all the time, but this isn't in your best interest. Many daily activities don't require much mental effort, which allows the mind to wander from the present moment and get into trouble. Examples include taking a shower, doing routine chores, commuting, and grocery shopping. None of these activities require constant thought; however, our minds often run nonstop during these times, wasting valuable energy that could be better used for something productive. Even worse, our vivid imaginations can take over, conjuring dreadful scenarios for the future (worry), replaying painful scenes from the past, and exaggerating everything that's wrong with the present. However, you can learn to quiet your mind during daily activities so it remains clear, composed, and ready to serve when needed.

When your mind is quiet, you can fully experience the most essential aspect of life—the present moment. This is because the mind often dwells on the past and the future instead of focusing on the present. The present moment is where all reality unfolds, and it is where your entire life happens. If you allow your mind to fixate on the past or the future, you miss out on your life.

Many people believe they need positive thoughts to experience peace, joy, and love—but this is not true. The richest and most wonderful feelings arise from a deep place that is largely independent of the thinking mind. You don't need to think joyful thoughts to feel joy, peaceful thoughts to feel peace, or loving thoughts to feel love. When the mind is still, you enter a state of rest that is sweeter than any positive thought, and this is accessible to everyone. This state of rest is neither dull nor empty—it is vibrant, expansive, and comforting.

Our minds tend to exaggerate the seriousness of situations beyond what is warranted, making life feel heavy and burdensome. By letting go of these thoughts, life feels lighter and less serious, allowing you to experience the fullness of the present instead of being lost in thought. When your normal state of mind is quiet, life begins to flow naturally, feeling more effortless and enjoyable.

Most people strive to enjoy life by learning to manage their finances, careers, and relationships. However, why do so few take the time to learn how to manage their thoughts and feelings? It's often assumed that everyone figures this out on their own, but in reality, very few people ever learn to effectively manage their thoughts and emotions or understand the importance of doing so. If you don't know how to manage your mind, life will always feel like a struggle. Managing your mind is even more important than managing your finances, career, or relationships, and it requires intentional practice and commitment.

Practice and commitment are essential for success in all areas of life—in some situations, they are vital for survival. If you've ever fallen off a raft or out of a canoe in fast-moving water, you've felt the helpless and perilous feeling of being swept along by the current. To get out of the water, you need to relax, point your feet downstream, and find a calm pool to swim out of and escape. If you plan to navigate treacherous waters, it's wise to practice this technique beforehand so you don't panic and risk drowning when you fall in.

The momentum of the thinking mind is like a fast-moving river, possessing the power to drag you along and engulf you. If you fall into its current and don't know how to escape, it will have to run its course before you can be free. It may take hours or even days for the mind to settle down once it gets going with anxious or angry thoughts. However, if you have practiced being mentally quiet, you'll be able to find a calm pool to escape to whenever you need it. In the next chapter, we will discuss how to practice this escape.

The thinking mind is a superb tool, but it can become a liability if it's allowed to run continuously. The thinking mind is *not* who you are—it is a tool that should be used constructively when needed and then set aside until required again.

Consider a vacuum cleaner: it makes noise and consumes energy, but no one leaves it running continuously. Its purpose is to clean carpets, and once you've finished using it, you unplug it and put it away. Imagine what your home would be like if the vacuum ran all day; you would feel perpetually frazzled, and no one would want to visit you.

If your mind is constantly running, you will find it difficult to fall asleep, even when you feel exhausted and frazzled. Sleep disorders are quite common, and excessive thinking is often a significant factor. To achieve a good night's sleep, it's essential to learn how to quiet your mind.

As mentioned earlier, sleep deprivation and chronic physical pain are closely linked. When you don't get enough sleep, your body's nervous system cannot settle down. Researchers have discovered that a lack of sleep leads to decreased levels of a neurotransmitter called NADA in a specific area of the brain. This decrease is associated with heightened pain sensitivity, a condition referred to as hyperalgesia.[23] Just as insufficient sleep can contribute to ongoing pain, chronic pain can also disrupt sleep, creating a vicious cycle where sleep deprivation acts as both a cause and a consequence of physical pain.

A mind that is constantly running will consume vast amounts of energy. Consider how you feel after spending a few hours studying for

---

23. https://www.medicalnewstoday.com/articles/how-sleep-loss-may-lead-to-heightened-pain-sensitivity, retrieved 5/28/25

an exam or preparing a detailed report for work. You feel tired even though you've been sitting the whole time. Similarly, if you attempt to study or work while sick with the flu, you can't do it because the energy just isn't there. You may notice that when you are ill, the repetitive mental chatter quiets down as your body conserves energy to fight the illness.

Repetitive negative thoughts (RNTs) consume energy and gradually drain your reserves. Many of these thoughts linger at the edges of your awareness, much like the constant hum of a fan that you've become accustomed to and no longer notice. Persistent thoughts about the past, the future, and dissatisfaction with the present slowly drain your energy because they never truly cease. This situation is similar to a slow leak in your car's gas tank that goes unnoticed until the tank is empty.

When you do stop this leak by quieting your mind, you will reclaim this energy. Your energy reservoir will begin to fill as the RNTs decrease. This is not the kind of energy measured in calories; rather, this is the energy you feel when you are enthusiastic about something. When you are full of enthusiasm, it doesn't matter if you've skipped a meal, and no obstacle can discourage you. The word "enthusiasm" originates from the Greek word "en-theos," meaning "full of God."

Trying to be mentally quiet is an uncomfortable experience for many people, especially in a culture that often values constant noise and activity. You might believe that it's impossible to stop thinking for more than a few seconds, or that attempting to do so is a waste of time or too boring to consider. Many individuals strongly identify with their thoughts—believing that their thoughts define who they are—which may lead to a fear of losing their sense of identity. Additionally, some have been taught in religious contexts that mental stillness is a dangerous Eastern practice that could invite negative influences, intensifying their fear.

French philosopher Blaise Pascal stated, "All of humanity's problems stem from man's inability to sit quietly in a room alone." We have been conditioned to fear silence, prompting us to fill our lives with distractions. This includes constant activity, frequently checking our phones, leaving the TV and radio on at all times, and becoming obsessively involved in hobbies and sports. Our culture and the technology we use have made this behavior both normal and accessible.

Reflect on why silence can feel uncomfortable and what you might fear about it. For many people, silence often brings up thoughts and feelings they'd rather avoid, so they drown them out with noise. Additionally, feelings of boredom can be unpleasant, prompting us to push them away rather than taking the time to explore what lies beneath them.

You may find temporary relief from mental noise by using drugs (both legal and illegal), alcohol, or engaging in dangerous or intense activities. Substances like drugs and alcohol can temporarily dull your mind, helping to suppress thoughts and emotions that you may wish to avoid. Activities such as mountain climbing, skydiving, and motorcycle racing demand complete focus on the present moment, effectively silencing any thoughts about the past or future. While these methods can offer short-term distractions for quieting the mind, they have significant risks and side effects.

Many safe and positive activities require a high level of focus that helps quiet the mind, and there's nothing wrong with that. One reason I enjoy off-road motorcycling in challenging terrain is that it requires my full attention and distracts me from other thoughts. The same goes for activities like skiing, playing video games, knitting a scarf, or completing a puzzle. However, it's important to recognize that these activities can also act as a form of suppression if they are used to avoid feeling emotional pain. Later, we will discuss more about the harmful effects of suppression and how this can lead to chronic physical pain.

You might have found relief from mental noise by becoming a workaholic. Your mind is so focused on constructive thoughts that it pushes aside the usual mental chatter. However, this comes at a high cost: it harms your relationships, neglects other aspects of life, and leads to exhaustion.

Your brilliant mind is meant for constructive work, but it can easily spiral out of control when you're not in charge. When the mind wanders into unproductive and repetitive thinking, it becomes a wicked master, transforming minor situations into major problems. However, when you gently take charge of your mind, it becomes a wonderful servant, making life's significant challenges seem much smaller.

Life is full of challenging situations, and one of the best ways to tackle a problem is to take a break and step away from it. *Creative solutions and insights often emerge when we are relaxed and not thinking about the issue.* Challenging situations require creativity, not just more thinking.

I first experienced this as a young engineering student while working late one night to debug a software program. I struggled to make sense of the problem, and nothing seemed to fit together. Eventually, I decided to give up, return to my dorm, and get some rest. However, just as I was walking out of the engineering building, a flash of insight struck me, and the solution became clear. I went back and completed the program in just a few minutes.

That moment stayed with me, and I've encountered similar situations countless times since. It took many years for this lesson to sink in, but I've learned that stepping away from a problem often leads to breakthroughs. This isn't always easy—the mind can be very stubborn, like a dog refusing to let go of a bone. In such cases, it's essential to gently take charge of your mind and insist on some relaxation.

When I get stuck and notice my thoughts becoming repetitive, I know it's time to let go and find a quiet place. I immediately get up from my desk and physically walk away from the problem when I'm at work. Walking away from the issue makes it seem smaller. I often repeat this process several times, periodically returning to the problem until the solution reveals itself. The brilliant Italian artist, inventor, and scientist, Leonardo da Vinci, expressed this in his journals:

> *"Every now and then go away, have a little relaxation, for when you come back to your work your judgment will be surer. Go some distance away because then the work appears smaller and more of it can be taken in at a glance and a lack of harmony and proportion is more readily seen."*

Resting the mind requires intention and discipline because it is like a freight train with a lot of momentum and no brakes. Once the mind gets going, it can be difficult to stop, leading you down a long path that ultimately leads to a dead end. Mental train wrecks happen when you eventually hit an impasse and experience deep frustration.

Relaxation can significantly boost your productivity by increasing your awareness. The more aware you are, the less time you waste pursuing dead ends and getting stuck on obstacles. Some have suggested that when you relax, your mind continues to think in the background, but I believe there is more to the story. The thinking mind creates tension and can lead to tunnel vision by focusing only on narrow perspectives, while awareness allows you to see the broader landscape. By taking time to relax and stepping back from active thought, you create space for awareness. This newfound awareness can reveal solutions that you were blind to when lost in thought.

Awareness is a distinct form of intelligence that goes beyond the thinking mind and is unencumbered by past conditioning. It has been said that "insanity is doing the same thing over and over again and expecting a different result." The thinking mind tends to apply the same old solutions to each problem, whereas awareness offers a fresh perspective on the broader picture.

Seeing problems from a new perspective is known as reframing. This process can occur when you discuss a problem with a colleague, friend, or therapist. However, it can also happen when you're alone if you take a moment to pause and quiet your mind. Achieving a quiet mind expands your awareness and brings clarity. This has become increasingly important in our society, as many businesses reduce staff to cut costs and individuals often work remotely across different time zones, solving problems in isolation. Humanity does not need more information or faster computers—it needs more quietude and awareness.

I am continually amazed by how most problems have elegant solutions that reveal themselves when I relax and create space for awareness. My creative engineering ideas often have little to do with my experience because awareness connects me with an intelligence greater than my limited thinking mind. Even the knottiest problems tend to work themselves out when I relax, allowing awareness to expand and creativity to flow. Recognizing this has not made me lazy; instead, it has given me the tenacity to keep revisiting seemingly hopeless problems when others are inclined to give up. I keep returning to them and thinking about them briefly until the solution appears. However, whenever I notice my thinking becoming circular or repetitive, I relax and quiet my mind. Just ten seconds of mental stillness or a short walk outdoors can often work wonders. I believe I am not unique in this—anyone can learn to be more creative and use their minds more effectively.

The most challenging problems often do not require creative solutions—*because they may not be real.* Many problems are merely constructs of the mind. When a mind driven by fear takes control, it can transform minor situations into seemingly hopeless dilemmas. This shift in perspective can lead to feelings of anxiety, anger, and depression.

I sometimes notice this tendency in myself first thing in the morning. Some days, I'm hit by a wave of anxiety or depression even before my feet touch the floor, often related to a situation at home or work. In the morning, my mind is hungry and seeks a problem to chew on—if necessary, it will even invent one. I've learned to smile and not take these feelings seriously, and I immediately begin my morning stillness practices. Once my mind is still and awareness starts to flow, these dark feelings retreat. These negative emotions do not represent my true self—they are a *false self* that pretends to be me but is not truly who I am. The false self cannot stand the light of awareness and will flee like a vampire when exposed to sunlight.

The practice of mental stillness, also known as meditation, is not some strange or mysterious trance—it is about becoming the manager of your mind. It involves learning to separate yourself from your thoughts instead of allowing them to control you. When you create distance from your thoughts, they lose their power over you and gradually quiet down.

Some religious traditions discourage meditation while also condemning worry, anger, hatred, unforgiveness, lust, greed, and judgment of others. *This presents a contradiction because if you are a slave to your thoughts and emotions, you are also enslaved by these vices.* Trying to rid yourself of these issues without learning to quiet your mind can be a futile exercise.

In the next chapter, we will explore how a daily quiet time can help you manage your mind and free you from the burden of constant and compulsive thinking—transforming darkness into the light of awareness.

Chapter 9

QUIET TIME

There are many ways to practice mental stillness, but the foundation involves spending a few minutes in quiet contemplation twice a day, every day. These brief periods of stillness promote a state of mental quiet throughout the day. The mind needs quiet time between thinking sessions to reset and recharge. As a result, your mind will feel rested and sharp when you need to use it, while negative thoughts and feelings will diminish. You will be amazed at what your mind is capable of when its baseline state is quiet.

At first, sitting quietly may feel like a chore, but once you experience the benefits, you will start to enjoy and crave these moments, making them your top priority. I suggest spending fifteen minutes twice a day; however, if this feels overwhelming, begin with just one minute per day and gradually increase the time from there. Every pathway to spiritual growth involves some daily quiet time. Just as successful athletes train regularly in the gym, authentic spiritual growth requires you to spend time in silence each day.

It's best to find a quiet environment for this practice. However, over time, you will discover that inner quiet does not depend on outer quiet, allowing you to practice anywhere.

Avoid reclining or lying down during your quiet time, as this signals to your body that it's time for sleep. Instead, choose a spot where you can maintain an upright posture, such as sitting in a chair or on the floor. Although sleeping and dreaming are vital for your well-being, they are automatic processes that serve a different purpose than quiet time. In contrast, the practice of mental stillness is not automatic; it requires a conscious effort on your part.

We've already discussed the tremendous power of expressive writing—also known as mechanical meditation. I often start my morning quiet time with a pen, paper, and a cup of coffee, writing down whatever is on my mind, no matter how private or uncomfortable those thoughts are. I also make sure to write again at the end of the day, just before going to bed. I suggest you do the same, as this simple practice can lead to significant progress.

Your daily quiet times should include a few minutes of sitting still with your eyes closed, noticing what's happening in your body, also known as inner-body awareness. Your attention cannot be in two places at once; therefore, as you direct your attention into your body, you pull focus away from your mind, allowing it to quiet down. You can practice this during your quiet times by noticing the sensations in your heart, belly, and gut. *Noticing* does not expend energy and create tension, unlike thinking or concentrating. You can *notice* things while remaining mentally relaxed.

The practice of mental stillness or meditation is *not* about concentration—it's about relaxed attention. Concentration is a highly focused form of thinking that uses energy and creates tension. Meditation, on the other hand, is the most relaxed state a person can be in without falling asleep.

Meditation is *not* about training your mind—it's about training your attention. Attention is directed toward feelings, the breath, and other body sensations instead of thoughts. Thoughts are allowed to pass by without getting lost in them—until they eventually fade away. The goal is to quiet your mind while remaining highly alert and aware.

When you sit quietly and relax, you may notice lingering feelings of anxiety, anger, or sadness in your chest, stomach, or gut caused by various situations in your life. You don't need to understand or label these feelings, as some can be difficult to identify. Instead, take a moment to explore your body, especially your chest and abdomen, simply to locate these feelings. Rather than trying to change or push them away—even if they feel uncomfortable—practice observing and welcoming them for a few minutes at a time. This approach, known as non-resistance, is the path of surrender, which we will cover in more detail later.

Your mind will try to feed and energize these feelings by attaching stories to them. Notice how these stories involve the past and future while rarely focusing on the present moment. If you are a visual thinker, you will visualize various mental images and movies. However, if you dwell on these images, you will become lost in thought. When this happens, gently return your attention to the sensations in your body, which helps draw attention away from your mind. Initially, you may need to repeat this often—perhaps every few seconds—as your mind tries to pull you into thinking about the past and future. However, with practice, you will learn to take charge and attend to your feelings more effectively as you settle into the present moment.

If you are experiencing physical pain and fatigue from not sleeping well, see if you can accept them for just one minute, rather than wishing they would go away. Fatigue is not an emotion, but like an emotion, you can learn to be comfortable with it instead of resisting it. Accepting physical pain is more challenging, but anything you can accept, even for a few seconds at a time, will be transformed into peace—this is the power of surrender.

If you feel restless, uneasy, or bored while trying to sit quietly, see if you can locate these sensations in your body. Instead of resisting them, allow these feelings to be present for a few minutes at a time. By relaxing and accepting these sensations, a small space will develop between you and them. When you become aware of this space, you are becoming the observer, which we'll explore further later.

If a noise interrupts your quiet time, such as a barking dog, a crying baby, or a ringing phone, notice how you instinctively react with irritation. When this happens, try to accept the noise and lean into the feeling of irritation. While you may feel compelled to express your displeasure, remember that each reaction reinforces that same response, making it more likely to occur again and intensify. It may be appropriate to address the disturbance, such as tending to the dog, baby, or phone, but do so gently. Accepting the situation and responding gently will lead to inner peace. Over time, these gentle responses during your quiet time will transform how you react to all of life, helping you overcome a lifetime of conditioned reactions.

Some religious traditions encourage meditating on a short verse of scripture or a sacred image to help displace negative thoughts and emotions. While practices like this can be helpful, you must *first* address your emotions. Ignoring this step may lead to emotional suppression, which can keep you stuck in pain by trapping your feelings in your body instead of letting them flow through you. The other consequences of suppressed emotions are well-known and can include increased anxiety, depression, and even a shorter lifespan.[24]

It's best to focus on the feelings in your body *before* contemplating a sacred verse or image. By acknowledging and accepting these feelings, you can allow them to flow freely and be released, instead of storing them away for later. The only way to be free from emotional pain—anxiety, fear, anger, regret, sadness, guilt, or any other emotion—is to go into it and experience it. This is the essence of the saying, "the way out is the way in."

If you cannot locate your feelings or feel nothing at all, direct your attention to the sensations of your breathing and notice your belly moving up and down. When you sit quietly, your breath becomes the most prominent sound in the room. Don't try to alter your breathing, relax and breathe naturally. When your mind starts to wander—and it will—gently guide your attention back to your breath and notice the air flowing in and out of your body, along with the sound it produces. As you practice this, you'll need to return to your breath many times, because the mind loves to chew on thoughts, much like dogs enjoy chewing on bones. The mind is always looking for something to chew on, but with practice, it will settle down, and you will take charge.

If watching your breath is a struggle, focus on just ten breaths at a time. Count each inhalation, then relax as you exhale after each count. Aim to relax a little more with each breath. If the mind wanders at any point, return to a count of one and start over. If you make it to ten—which can be tough at first—then go back to one and keep going. This is similar to going to the gym and lifting weights in sets of ten repetitions; one solid set of ten reps can make a significant difference.

---

24. https://pubmed.ncbi.nlm.nih.gov/24119947/ PMCID: PMC3939772 retrieved 5/24/25

Breathing is unique among bodily functions because it happens automatically while still allowing for conscious control. Intentionally manipulating your breath can be helpful in specific situations, and we will explore this further later. However, during my quiet time, I prefer to observe the automatic process rather than trying to change it. I focus on the stillness in the silent gaps between breaths and wait in anticipation for each new breath. Breathing often slows down and deepens when you relax, so I pay attention to how it gradually changes on its own. The entire process is quite amazing when you truly observe what's happening. This practice tends to capture my full attention, which pulls focus away from my mind, making it very quiet.

Your first attempts at sitting quietly and observing your feelings or breath will likely leave you feeling frustrated and thinking that you can't do this. You may experience a whirlwind of intrusive thoughts, a nagging fear haunting you, constant distractions, and a voice that says, "You are wasting time." Fortunately, there is no such thing as a bad quiet time. Even advanced meditators face these distractions and repeatedly bring their attention back to their body again and again. This is an essential part of the exercise, just like repeating sets at the gym, even when you feel like a weakling. Each time you gently return your attention to your body, you build your "presence power," which is your ability to stay present and aware instead of being lost in thought. The cycle of wandering into thought and then returning to a state of presence is not a failure; it is a vitally important part of the process and must be approached with patience and self-forgiveness. Remember, this isn't a battle—if you fight against your mind, you will lose.

With daily practice, a similar cycle will naturally begin unfolding throughout the day. You will notice your attention fully absorbed by thought, and then periodically return it to a state of rest. In this manner, constructive thinking sessions become more effective because they are interspersed with quiet moments, allowing the mind to reset and awareness to flow. This is like hitting the restart button on your computer to resolve sluggish behavior and crashes. Periodic restarts will enhance the performance and stability of both you and your computer.

If everything is going well in your life, you might find yourself caught in a whirlwind of positive thoughts when you try to sit quietly.

Perhaps your bank account is growing, you're planning the ultimate vacation, or your child just came home with straight A's on their report card. There's nothing wrong with positive thinking—it certainly feels good. However, focusing too much on these positive thoughts won't help you build your "presence power."

Your quiet time is for growing, and ruminating over positive thoughts—also known as clinging—will not lead to growth. Life will inevitably present situations where your negative thoughts run over your positive thoughts like a steamroller, so you must practice separating from *all* of your thoughts. In all cases, this is achieved by noticing the sensations in your body or observing your breath, and by refraining from dwelling on mental stories, even if they are pleasant. You will find that separating from pleasant thoughts can be just as challenging as separating from dark thoughts. Remember that beneath your thoughts and emotions—pleasant or otherwise—lies something much deeper, richer, and sweeter than anything your mind can provide.

Your "presence power" will initially develop slowly, often without any noticeable progress. It's essential to let go of expectations for rapid change and to refrain from labeling your quiet time as good or bad. Building presence power can sometimes feel like trying to train cats, because it's easy for attention to be drawn away by thoughts and external distractions. This process requires persistence. Some days will be more challenging than others, and at times you may find yourself completely lost in thought. However, remember that this is an ongoing investment, similar to maintaining a regular gym routine.

If you stick with it, you will eventually take charge of your mind instead of being its slave, and you will see benefits in every area of your life. You will find that these few minutes of quiet will do far more to restore your energy than any power nap, and it won't leave you feeling groggy. You will avoid making mistakes because your mind will be well-rested and ready for service when needed, *and* you will be more aware. Your productivity and creativity will improve along with your ability to focus and listen. You won't need constant activity to escape the tyranny of the mind because you'll have the power to drop repetitive negative thoughts (RNTs) at will. A lifetime of programmed reactions will unravel, and your physical and emotional pain will subside.

If you establish a daily quiet time and stay consistent, you will notice one day that a space has formed between you and your emotions. This realization might happen on an ordinary day when something triggers a reaction within you, but instead of feeling overwhelmed, you'll perceive it as if you are watching the reaction in someone else. This space signifies that you are becoming a silent observer—a concept we will explore further in the next chapter.

Chapter 10

THE SILENT OBSERVER

You cannot force your mind to slow down, because *it is* like a freight train that has a throttle but no brakes. The only way to stop a train without a brake is to let go of the throttle and allow it to coast to a stop gradually. Similarly, thoughts and feelings have a lot of momentum and are not easily stopped, so when the mind starts racing, you must let go of *its* throttle. This means relaxing and not trying to fix or change unwelcome thoughts; instead, you allow them to be and simply leave them alone. You navigate life while observing emotional disturbances flow through you instead of identifying with them. This practice is called being the silent observer or the silent watcher.

Psychotherapist and spiritual teacher, Anthony de Mello, described feeling depressed before he became enlightened, but strangely, he said he continued to feel depressed at times afterward. However, there was a *big* difference—he was able to step outside the depression and observe it without identifying with it. He stopped trying to make it go away and was perfectly happy to go on with his life as the depression passed through him. If you are experiencing depression and this perspective doesn't resonate with you yet, take heart—it means you have something wonderful to look forward to.[25]

We all have "invisible hands" inside us that we use to push away uncomfortable thoughts and feelings, or cling to pleasant ones. When you become the silent observer, you stop using these hands to push or cling. Instead, you place these hands behind you and gently fold their fingers together, making them unavailable. This way, thoughts and feelings are allowed to be, and you don't touch them. Once you touch

---

25. Anthony De Mello, Awareness, p. 59

a thought, you can easily become lost in it. The silent observer—your true self—lets go and remains uninvolved, knowing that thoughts and feelings do not define your true essence.

It's natural to identify with thoughts and feelings, but the problem is that when you identify with a thought, you cannot observe it objectively because you have merged with it. There is no space for you to step back and watch. It has become part of a false identity that you've created. However, that false identity or false self is not you—it's a phantom that pretends to be you. When you learn to disidentify from the false self, some space will open up inside, allowing you to observe thoughts and feelings as if they were happening to someone else.

This space will be tenuous if you become involved and attach stories to your feelings. Being a silent observer means avoiding mental commentary on the feelings you observe. It's natural to attach sad stories, angry stories, and scary stories to your feelings in the form of repetitive mental conversations and mental movies. If someone cheated or betrayed you, the incident may replay in your mind hundreds of times and become more dramatic each time. When you replay these mental stories, you feed the feelings that accompany them. When you feed negative feelings, they grow stronger and will continue to resurface. They become like those pesky geese and ducks in the park; it's natural to want to feed them, but if you keep feeding them, they will never go away.

I recommend practicing observing your feelings before attempting to observe your thoughts. Thoughts and feelings often go hand in hand—like lightning and thunder—but this isn't always the case. For instance, you might feel anxious without being aware of the underlying thoughts, just as you can hear thunder without seeing the lightning that caused it. Thoughts can flash through your mind quickly, much like lightning, while feelings tend to linger, akin to the rumble of thunder. Because feelings stick around longer, they are often easier to observe than thoughts, and it is the energy of these feelings that needs to be released.

If a negative thought or feeling requires action, it's essential to take the necessary steps or plan to do so, then refocus your attention on the accompanying feelings if they persist. If it's a complicated situation or a relationship problem, and you don't know what to do, stay with the feeling as much as possible so you don't feed the thought and identify with it. This will give your awareness room to expand. Once you create some space for awareness, the action you need to take will become clear.

In my experience, most negative thoughts and feelings don't actually require any action. Instead, all you need to do is sit with the feelings in your body, allowing them to flow through you and be released. Initially, as you learn this process, the emotional energy may move slowly, much like water percolating through sand. However, as you learn to relax more deeply and release this energy, it will begin to flow more freely.

The energy of emotions like anxiety, anger, and grief can be very uncomfortable, prompting a natural desire to push them away and seek something more pleasant. *However, it is not necessary to replace negative thoughts with positive ones.* Instead, you can choose to be present and aware, allowing these emotions to flow through you. While positive thinking is often celebrated in our culture, it does not address the root of the issue. In fact, positive thinking can subtly act as a form of suppression, indicating a refusal to confront one's pain. When you suppress thoughts and feelings, you inadvertently give them more power, causing them to grow stronger. This is why the saying goes, "what you resist, persists."

The mind tends to amplify thoughts when we attempt to suppress them. Fyodor Dostoevsky noted this phenomenon in 1863 in his essay "Winter Notes on Summer Impressions." He wrote, "Try to pose for yourself this task: do not think of a polar bear, and you will see that the cursed thing will come to mind every minute." Over a century later, social psychologist Daniel Wegner tested this idea in a laboratory setting, known as "The White Bears Experiment." He instructed participants not to think about white bears and asked them to ring a bell if such a thought occurred. Despite these instructions, participants thought about white bears, on average, once per minute. Suppressing their thoughts about white bears reinforced the thought, causing it to occur more frequently.

We all experience thoughts that are more disturbing than white bears and that we prefer to avoid, so it's natural to try to push them away. However, this is exactly the wrong approach. When you resist the flow of life, which includes your thoughts and feelings, you become less receptive to the flow of grace. The path to freedom lies in learning to be comfortable with those thoughts and feelings and welcoming them instead of fighting against them. Even the most troubling feelings must be permitted if you want to be free of them—this is the practice of non-resistance or acceptance.

Suppressed feelings can create a buildup of emotional trash that accumulates over a lifetime. This buildup of trash is unstable, much like the magma beneath a dormant volcano, just waiting for an opportunity to erupt and cause trouble. Suppressed feelings from the past often erupt as overreactions to minor situations in the present, such as when you "fly off the handle" because you misplaced your keys. However, when these feelings *do* rise to the surface—and they eventually will—you can learn to relax and observe them quietly. As you practice silently observing distressing feelings, their energy will gradually dissipate from your stockpile and will no longer trouble you. Remember that this doesn't happen overnight—you must be patient and work on it each day.

Releasing your stockpile of emotional trash means *relaxing* instead of resisting. You release a negative feeling by relaxing into it, just as you relax into and welcome a happy feeling. This "leaning into the pain" allows the energy to pass through you instead of sticking around and becoming part of a false identity. Relaxation is the key—however, you cannot relax if you attach stories to your feelings. *You must drop the stories to relax.* There is no limit to how deeply you can relax; even if you think you've relaxed as much as possible, strive to relax even deeper.

Relaxation and non-resistance can be illustrated through the concept of Chinese handcuffs, also known as finger traps. These toys are made of braided tubes that tighten around your fingers when you try to pull them apart. The more you struggle to remove them, the tighter they become. The only way to free your fingers is to stop pulling and relax your hands.

Non-resistance applies to both emotional and physical pain. If you've ever had a migraine headache, you know that fighting against it only makes the pain worse. I've been in situations where I had to push through a migraine, and I experienced a horrible escalation of symptoms that's hard to describe. Even modern medications for migraines, like Sumatriptan, are ineffective if you keep resisting the pain. Instead, it's essential to slow down, relax, and find a quiet place to stop fighting. Confronting severe pain is challenging—it's like facing a raging fire. But as strange as it may sound, I've learned that turning toward the pain—instead of turning away—is the best way to move past it. I will discuss intense physical pain in more detail in Chapter 23.

When you face a major emotional upheaval, such as losing your job or ending a relationship, it may be necessary to observe your feelings for an extended period while letting go of the associated story. This process might take a few days or even longer, but as you become comfortable with these feelings, a space will open up and awareness will emerge. This will let you ask questions like, "Why am I doing this to myself?" or "What is the point of all this upset?" or "Will this really matter in the long run?" If you can maintain that inner space, the energy of the upsetting experience will pass through you and eventually leave.

That said, if you attempt to observe a significant emotional disturbance without first practicing with more minor issues, you will likely become frustrated. It's like picking up a new musical instrument for the first time and expecting to play beautiful music. It requires practice, and you need to work on it daily, starting with minor irritations. However, if you have practiced with the small things, you will be surprised one day at how easily you handle something big.

If you're facing a seemingly hopeless problem and are searching for an answer, it will arrive when you become a silent observer. This is because awareness flows when you are relaxed and allow your feelings to be, rather than through constant thinking. Awareness acts as a floodlight that illuminates darkness, connecting you with an intelligence far greater than your limited mind. Even the most hopeless situations have elegant solutions or can be accepted as they are when viewed from a different perspective.

In the next chapter, we will learn about a simple tool that can empower you to become a silent observer, even when a surge of reactive energy threatens to overwhelm you.

Chapter 11

ISN'T THAT INTERESTING?

During my college days, I attended a stage performance by a professional hypnotist named James Mapes. He had performed several times on campus and was quite popular among the students. Out of curiosity and for pure entertainment, I decided to attend his show one evening, and what I witnessed was truly bizarre. He could temporarily transform a Democrat into a Republican simply by suggesting it to the subject's subconscious mind. The fully awake political convert would then passionately defend his new viewpoint as if he genuinely believed it, until Mapes reversed the suggestion. It was so strange that I initially thought some parts must have been staged. However, to my surprise, one of my typically reserved engineering friends stood up and began dancing in the aisle after being influenced by a suggestion.

The day after the show, I attended a small seminar that Mapes led on campus, and I was further impressed by his ability to influence people's subconscious thinking. I remember feeling deeply unsettled by how fragile and susceptible our minds can be. The subconscious mind is a mysterious realm that cannot be directly observed, yet it profoundly influences all of our thoughts and behaviors. Many of the automatic thoughts we have today were programmed into our subconscious in the past and have little to do with present reality.

Thirty years after graduating from college, as I began learning how to be a silent observer, I discovered that James Mapes had written a popular book titled *Imagine That*. I knew this book would provide valuable insights into the workings of the human mind, so I was eager to read it. One favorite technique he teaches for becoming an observer of your thoughts and feelings is to verbalize three specific words whenever you notice your mind spiraling with negative thoughts. The three simple words are *"Isn't that interesting?"*[26] It may sound too simple, but I have found that saying these three words out loud has significantly improved the quality of my life.

How can three words possibly change someone's life? While the words themselves may not create change, expressing them brings awareness to the mind's dysfunction and helps you disassociate from it. The question creates a pause that allows your true self to make a deliberate choice instead of reacting. These three words also anchor you in the present moment, enabling you to observe your thoughts rather than being consumed by them. When you become the observer of your thoughts, you create space and distance from them, preventing the false self from gaining a foothold within you. The idea of creating space instead of reacting to a situation is reflected in this well-known quote, commonly attributed to Viktor E. Frankl, a psychiatrist and Holocaust survivor.

"Between stimulus and response, there is a space. In that space is our power to choose our response. In our response lies our growth and our freedom."

I remember the first time I used this three-word strategy. I was returning a rental car at an airport in Montana, feeling very tired and stressed. Being very conscientious, I always make it a point to walk around and inspect the vehicle for any damage before returning the keys. If I have time, I even try to wash it thoroughly beforehand.

As I walked around the car, I noticed scratches on the paint that hadn't been there when I picked it up. A sense of dread washed over me, and I began to berate myself for not being more careful and for not having purchased the extra insurance. I started to envision the worst-case scenario, where I would be charged thousands of dollars to have the car repainted. Standing there in the airport parking lot, my agitation grew, and my mind raced with anxious thoughts.

---

26. Mapes, Imagine That, p 48

I walked away from the car feeling upset and angry with myself. However, I decided to focus on my emotions and said out loud in the middle of the parking lot, *"Isn't that interesting?"* This statement interrupted the flow of negative thoughts that were feeding my feelings. In less than a minute, my anger and frustration lifted, and a sense of lightness washed over me as I dropped off the keys and walked into the airport. The scratches on the rental car now seemed like a very small problem, and in the end, I wasn't charged for the damage.

The three simple words, *"Isn't that interesting?"* helped me detach from my negative thoughts and feelings, allowing me to observe them more objectively. By becoming a silent observer, I was able to relax, which in turn expanded my awareness and enabled me to view my situation more objectively. My true self could then see the reality of the situation, which was a minor problem that was unlikely to turn into anything significant—and it didn't.

This technique serves as a valuable tool for helping you disidentify from your mind rather than fighting against it. Unlike expressive writing, this method doesn't require pen and paper. You can gently whisper these three words whenever you notice the voice in your head speaking negativity, fear, or self-doubt. Hardly a day passes without my using these three powerful words.

The false self tends to magnify minor issues and transform them into catastrophes. However, most of the challenges we encounter are relatively insignificant when viewed within the larger scope of life and the short time we have here. Why squander precious moments getting upset over something trivial when our time is so limited? Very often, I find myself saying out loud, *"Isn't that interesting?"* and following it up with, *"This is a very small problem."*

It's best to say these words out loud so they can flow from your mouth, travel back through your ears, and into your brain, where they can be recorded as new input. The spoken word carries great power, but if you try to do this silently in your head, you're just creating thoughts that chase other thoughts, like sending a phantom to pursue another phantom. Later, we'll see how carefully selected positive statements spoken aloud—known as affirmations—can help reprogram your subconscious and bring about significant changes.

Change doesn't always happen quickly, and some emotional disturbances can linger for a very long time. However, when you take on the role of a silent observer, these emotions lose their power to bother you. I am reminded of this truth each time I walk my dog and he does his business on a neighbor's lawn. In those moments, I have to pick up after him and carry the poop bag with me for a while. Although it's not pleasant to carry something like that, it doesn't bother me because it's contained in a small bag, separate from me. Similarly, when you are the silent observer of your emotions, you can carry your emotional trash just like that little bag—you are aware of it, but it remains separate and contained, so that it no longer stinks.

Your true self—which is the silent observer—does not change moment to moment as your thoughts and feelings do. Your true self serves as the channel for peace, joy, and love, which run deeper than and beyond emotions. Your true self understands that automatic thoughts and feelings will do what they do and does not take them seriously. When you learn to dwell in your true self, it won't matter to you what your mind and emotions are doing; you will observe them and may even smile at them as you rest in a much higher place.

Abiding in this higher place, where you are present and aware, is called "being centered." You can learn to re-center yourself, regardless of any disturbances that come along. This higher place of rest is what everyone is looking for—unfortunately, most people look for it externally rather than within themselves.

Chapter 12

THE FALSE SELF VS. AWARENESS

The human mind can be a wonderful servant, but it can turn against you and become a wicked master. The wicked master is the voice in your head that continually reminds you of painful moments from your past, your deepest fears about the future, and everything that seems wrong in the present. When you identify with this voice, it becomes your false identity or false self. The false self has many names—the ego, the lower self, or the sinful nature—and it possesses the power to enslave you and ruin your life. However, when you learn to disidentify from the false self, it marks the beginning of a new life.

The false self is a constructed persona that manifests as automatic thoughts, feelings, and reactions. These include worries, insecurities, attachments, judgments, compulsions, resentment, guilt, and more. In most cases, you don't choose to have these—they happen automatically and are the product of your experiences, which develop unconsciously. While these thoughts and feelings might seem like you, they are not truly who you are. They are merely phantoms masquerading as you, creating a false identity.

The process of disidentifying with the false self is sometimes referred to as "losing the self" or "dying to the self." You cannot fight the false self—you can only free yourself from it by observing it. When you learn to become the observer of these negative thoughts and feelings, some space will form inside you, allowing you to separate from them. With this space, you become aware of the useless and sometimes toxic nature of your automatic thoughts and feelings. This awareness produces a knowing that they are not who you are, so you disassociate from them, and they no longer control you. When you disidentify with your mind, it becomes a wonderful servant instead of a wicked master.

The most important question you will ever ask is "Who am I?" It is natural to identify with your thoughts, but thinking is something you do, and your thoughts are not the essence of who you are. Thoughts come and go—but you are always there—noticing them. Thoughts trigger feelings, which also have a fleeting nature. When you feel angry or frightened, you are the knower of these feelings—not the feelings that are known. Transitory thoughts and feelings cannot be you, because you are always there, experiencing them.

You are the consciousness or true self that exists beneath the fluctuating thoughts and feelings. You are the one who welcomes pleasant thoughts and feelings while pushing away uncomfortable ones. You can learn to notice your thoughts and feelings without identifying with them, which allows you to separate from them and enhance your awareness.

Awareness flows from your true self and is closer to the essence of who you truly are. Awareness is not the same as thinking, because when you are lost in thought, you cease to be aware. Awareness expands when you can notice things without thinking about them. Noticing without thinking keeps you anchored in the present, instead of being consumed by thoughts of the past and future. Noticing transitions into thinking when you resist what you don't like or cling to what you do like.

"Likes" and "dislikes" create a constant stream of mental commentary that feeds into the automatic and repetitive thinking of the false self. Both "likes" and "dislikes" are forms of judgment, as they involve evaluating what "should be" or what "should not be." Most of the time, we remain unaware of this and fall into an endless cycle of preferences, aversions, labels, opinions, and a variety of other programmed thoughts and reactions. This persistent mental noise does not benefit you or others and significantly drains your energy. By learning to quiet your mind, you can reclaim this energy and channel it into something constructive.

All thinking requires energy and can create tension, but awareness flows when you are relaxed. *Always strive to relax into your thoughts and feelings, no matter how distressing they may be.* This approach helps you cultivate awareness and become the observer of your false self. If you fight against your mind, you will remain its slave—if you relax, you will gently take charge.

Awareness should not be confused with alertness; even a house fly is alert, and you are much more than a house fly. While awareness includes alertness, it goes much deeper than that.

Awareness is a form of understanding that goes beyond mere intellectual knowledge and transcends the mind's past conditioning. Unfortunately, for many individuals, this deeper awareness often emerges only after they have experienced suffering. For instance, alcoholics may know that excessive drinking is harmful, but true awareness typically arises only when they find themselves lying in a filthy gutter. Similarly, cigarette smokers understand that smoking causes lung cancer, but until their doctor shows them the tumor on their lung X-ray, there is no real awareness. While awareness alone may not be sufficient to overcome such addictions, it is undoubtedly a crucial first step.

To knowingly consume poison is, at best, foolish and, at worst, insane. The New England home where I grew up had a well, and we later discovered that the groundwater contained arsenic. Once we became aware of the arsenic, we stopped drinking the well water.

Human beings often worry about things beyond their control, which brings no benefits and can seriously harm their well-being— much like consuming poison. Awareness connects you to reality and enables you to release toxic thoughts that can drain your energy and make you ill. Often, increased awareness is all that's necessary to achieve freedom from these thoughts and the feelings they trigger.

If you could experience pure awareness, you would see the world as it truly is, rather than through a cloudy and distorted lens. Your past conditioning heavily influences the thinking mind, while awareness separates you from your past, offering a fresh and new perspective. Awareness has been called "seeing the light." However, awareness is not a spotlight—it is a floodlight that illuminates the big picture of your whole life.

Awareness extends beyond your individual experience. It enables you to see life from others' perspectives, fostering empathy, compassion, forgiveness, and love. Complete and pure awareness embodies the all-knowing, the omniscient, or the Divine.

Awareness allows you to recognize the issues that hinder your growth. In engineering, we often say that "understanding the problem is ninety percent of the solution." This is because when you truly grasp the problem, finding the solution typically becomes straightforward. It's common to blame your difficulties on external factors, but the reality is that the actual problem lies within you. Your mind transforms situations into problems, so it's not the external circumstances that trouble you—*it's your mind's reaction to them*. Nothing outside of you has the power to disturb you; only your mind can do that. No one can make you feel angry or anxious; that power resides solely within your mind. You are entirely responsible for your thoughts, including any bitterness or resentment you may harbor, regardless of what others have said or done. While your ability to change the external world and influence other people is limited, your capacity to improve your inner self is limitless.

If you are searching for peace, happiness, and love outside of yourself, you are pursuing unobtanium, which is something that doesn't truly exist. The world and any relationship cannot provide these feelings in a lasting way. Don't fall for the misconception that you will be okay once today's big problem is resolved or when you meet the right person. There will always be a multitude of problems waiting in line to trouble you, and the next issue will quickly take the place of the previous one if you allow it to. Why let your thoughts and feelings be controlled by external circumstances over which you have little influence? Instead, focus on the inner work, where you have complete control. Why not relax and appreciate every moment, including the difficult ones? When you learn to make this choice, you will discover a freedom and inner joy that is deeper and more fulfilling than anything the outside world can provide.

Finding this freedom is much like learning a new sport. A certain amount of consistent practice is necessary, but unlike most sports, no special talent is required. All you need is the desire to be free from enslavement to the mind. When learning a new sport like skiing, you expect to fall, so you start on the bunny slope instead of the steep black diamond trails. Similarly, as you learn to gently take charge of your mind, you should begin with the small situations that trigger those automatic thoughts and feelings. This is, in effect, allowing life to be your teacher. Every situation presents an opportunity to expand your awareness and let go of the false self you've created. If you practice daily with these small situations, you will be amazed at how big situations can no longer affect you.

If you drive a car, you can start allowing life be your teacher today. The next time you find yourself stuck in traffic or when someone cuts you off, remind yourself to stop drinking the poison by saying out loud, "There is zero benefit to getting agitated, but there is a significant cost to my well-being."

Instead of getting caught up in the mental stories about being late, criticizing other drivers, or wondering why there's never a cop around when you need one, focus on the feelings of agitation in your body. This may be challenging at first—you'll probably feel the urge to push the agitation away or reinforce it with more mental narratives.

Instead, gently redirect your attention to the sensations of agitation in your body. When you do this, your mind will naturally slow down, as your attention cannot focus on two things at once. Each time your thoughts start to spiral, relax and bring your attention back to the physical sensations of agitation in your body. By not resisting the agitation, you will begin to separate from it, allowing it to pass through you slowly. Just as with your daily quiet time, allowing life to be your teacher isn't about training your mind—it's about training your attention.

If you manage to overcome the agitation, you may experience boredom while stuck in traffic. Boredom is uncomfortable and has been called "the mind's hunger" because the mind craves a stimulus that is not being satisfied. This hunger can be a positive force when it motivates you to work and serve others instead of being lazy, but it can also cause unnecessary suffering. You could add some positive mental distractions, such as music or an audiobook, to feed your mind, or you could simply acknowledge the boredom. If you can notice and accept the boredom, a space will form around it, and you will become the observer of it. If you can be okay with the boredom for a while, it will pass through you, revealing the deep ocean of peace beneath it.

When you reach the point where you can relax and fully accept your agitation or boredom, you will transition into a state of presence. In this state, there is a space between you and your emotions, and your mind is relatively quiet. You are aware of everything around you, but are not adding mental commentary. You will feel relaxed and at peace, perceiving the world through a wide-angle lens, rather than fixating on specific things and letting your mind turn them into problems.

If you practice this regularly, you'll arrive late to work one day amidst heavy traffic but feel relaxed and energized instead of tense and drained. This experience isn't just a pipe dream—it is achievable for anyone who wants to break free from enslavement to the mind.

Don't be surprised or disappointed if this doesn't happen and you end up "losing it" the first time you try. An athlete doesn't go to the gym for the first time and bench press five hundred pounds—he starts with a much lighter weight and gradually builds his strength. Similarly, life will throw five-hundred-pounders at you that you won't be able to handle. You must practice daily with lighter situations to gradually build your ability to stay present and aware instead of getting lost in thought and reactivity.

The practice of allowing life to be your teacher should be complemented by a daily quiet time (see Chapter 9). Your quiet time is like an athlete lifting lighter weights at the gym, while allowing life to teach you is like competing against a tough opponent. By adding quiet time to your routine, you'll find that your presence power grows steadily, enabling you to handle life's disturbances without reacting.

If all this seems too complicated, don't get discouraged. The path to freedom from physical and psychological pain is quite simple. It's as straightforward as pressing the delete key on your computer to remove unwanted text. In truth, spiritual growth and liberation from pain doesn't come from *adding* anything to your life—it comes from *subtracting* what stands in the way. Let us delve further into the topic of subtraction in the next chapter.

Chapter 13

SUBTRACTION

M eister Eckhart, the late 13th-century Christian mystic, wrote, "God is not found in the soul by adding anything, but by a process of *subtraction*." Spiritual growth is not about gaining, attaining, or achieving—it's about removing mental and emotional clutter to uncover the deep ocean of peace, joy, and love that lies beneath.

The principle of subtraction is illustrated in the well-known Parable of the Sower.[27] In this parable, seeds sown in good soil cannot grow and bear fruit because they are choked by thorns. The thorns symbolize worries and attachments to material things. Just like seeds in good soil, all *you* need to do is remove the thorns that are blocking your growth. Everything necessary for your growth is already within you—*there's no need to add anything*.

Worries and attachments greatly contribute to the mind's useless and toxic thought patterns, which we will examine in detail later. Therefore, when you learn to let them go, your mind will quiet down considerably. In that stillness, you will find a new sense of peace, and within that peace, a subtle joy will emerge. These feelings of peace and joy are not emotions because emotions are usually tied to thinking. Instead, they transcend thought and emotion, rising from a much deeper place within you.

You may have been taught to trust your emotions or to follow your heart or gut feelings, but doing so can lead to trouble. Emotions aren't inherently bad; when correctly managed, they are an essential and beautiful part of the human experience. However, it's important to

---

27. Mt 13:1-23

understand that thoughts and emotions are different. Thoughts occur quickly and can change rapidly, while emotions have a certain momentum and tend to linger, especially if you feed them with more thoughts.

Suppressing your emotions only makes things worse, as it puts them in long-term storage, causing them to resurface later and trouble you even more. Some deeply ingrained emotions can persist for years, triggering automatic thoughts and reactions that are often misguided and disconnected from present reality. As a result, trusting your emotions can lead you to draw false conclusions about a situation or yourself. This phenomenon is known as "emotional reasoning," which we will explore later. That's why the advice to trust your feelings or to follow your heart can be misleading. It's akin to making investment decisions today based on last year's financial news. Emotions can be way out of sync with reality and should not serve as your primary guide.

Emotions are not the same as intuition, even though both can create a feeling in your gut. Intuition, like awareness, arises from your true self and is not the product of thinking or reasoning. Intuition is much deeper and more subtle than emotion, and it can serve as a helpful guide. However, intuition is easily colored by your thoughts and feelings, so you must learn to distinguish it from "emotional reasoning." When you become the observer of your thoughts and emotions instead of identifying with them, it becomes easier to recognize and trust your intuition.

Emotions such as anxiety and rage should be viewed as emotional trash, and it's best to subtract them from your life. In contrast, uncomfortable feelings like grief and remorse are essential. Grief, in particular, reflects the love for someone who is no longer with you, and love is always healthy. If you have lost a loved one, it's completely normal and healthy to grieve for an extended period.

However, be cautious, as your false self may try to make you identify with your grief, leading you to say things like, "a part of me has died," or "I will never be happy again." This identification with grief can potentially lead to depression.

Remorse is an uncomfortable emotion that arises from making a mistake or a poor choice. However, this feeling can be positive because it increases your awareness of how your words and actions impact others. Healthy remorse motivates you to change and make amends when possible. Conversely, if you focus excessively on past mistakes and allow this feeling to define you, remorse can turn into guilt—a persistent sense of self-condemnation that may last for years.

To grow spiritually, it's essential to treat all your feelings with equal regard, which means welcoming them, even when they're uncomfortable. It may seem counterintuitive to accept negative emotions like anxiety or rage that you ultimately want to eliminate, but accepting them is the surest way to free yourself from them.

When you can welcome, or at least accept, an uncomfortable feeling, you'll create an internal space that allows you to observe it, which helps it lose its hold on you. To maintain the role of observer, you must practice experiencing the feeling in your body without getting caught up in mental narratives. If you feed the feeling with a story, that internal space will close up, and your false self will take control.

The false self can be relentless—to be completely free of it, you must learn to surrender. Surrender is not easy, but it is the highest path. Surrender is not about making everything okay—*it's about being okay with everything as it is*. When you are okay with everything, your mind and emotions have little to say, and a deep stillness settles within.

A person who surrenders gives their best in every situation, yet does not allow specific outcomes to dictate their well-being. They align themselves with how things are, instead of how they believe things should be, and do not resist the flow of life. Although surrender may sound like weakness, it is anything but that. Surrender unleashes great power and arises from a broad perspective on life and an awareness of the temporary nature of all things.

It's essential to understand that surrender is neither laziness, indifference, nor inaction. On the contrary, surrender involves taking action when necessary and responding appropriately to the present moment without reacting impulsively.

The false self believes that its strength comes from resisting life and trying to force things to happen the way it wants. *However, the truth is that resistance is a form of weakness and fear disguised as strength.* This becomes evident when you accept a situation you were previously resisting—you realize that you were confronting your fears. Since the false self is built on resistance, embracing non-resistance causes the false self to dissolve. Non-resistance is the key to true freedom and strength.

The terms "non-resistance," "acceptance," and "surrender" are closely related, and I often use them interchangeably. However, for some people, these words can trigger automatic reactions based on past experiences, and the words themselves can create resistance. Words like "surrender" and "acceptance" might evoke feelings of weakness or giving up. If this is the case for you, consider using the term "allow" instead of "accept" or "surrender." *Allowing* things to be as they are is a conscious choice made from a position of strength.

Learning to surrender and becoming an observer goes beyond intellectual concepts—it requires *practice* to truly understand them. Reality cannot be grasped solely through words and ideas; it must be experienced firsthand. For example, you can't know what Coca-Cola tastes like just by studying its ingredients or hearing others talk about it. To truly understand the flavor of Coca-Cola, you need to take a sip and experience it yourself. Only through experiencing something can you truly know it. Once you've taken that sip, the ingredients and descriptions become less important—you'll know what it is.

Words can serve as pointers or signposts to what is real, but that is their limitation. Try describing the fragrance of a rose using words—it cannot be done. If words fail to capture the essence of a single rose's fragrance, how can they possibly convey the infinite nature of the Divine? You cannot dissect a pointer and discover the truth; the truth lies in what the pointer points to, not in the pointer itself. The finger that points to the moon is not the moon; you cannot study the finger to understand the moon. Once you experience the reality to which words and concepts point, their importance diminishes.

Spirituality points to what exists beyond the mind, but articulating it with words can be particularly challenging. It is easy to define misery, as it originates in the mind; however, defining joy is more difficult because joy arises from beyond the mind. This is why spiritual teachings often emphasize the mind's dysfunction and say less about what lies beyond it. The only way to truly know what exists beyond the mind is to experience it for yourself.

The mind tends to reduce everything to words and labels, which can distort our perception of reality. I enjoy birdwatching, and when I travel, I sometimes spot a bird I don't recognize. This is exciting because seeing a new creature for the first time sparks a sense of child-like wonder and awe. However, my mind wants to identify the new bird and give it a label. Once I learn the name, my perception shifts. Part of the initial wonder and awe is lost because the label creates a barrier between me and the experience. Jiddu Krishnamurti summed this up when he said, "The day you teach a child the name of a bird, the child will never see that bird again." When we label something, we act as if we fully understand it, but in truth, we don't. The mind labels everything, including people, with words like jerk, idiot, fool, loser, great guy, or hero. This labeling is a form of overgeneralization that disconnects us from reality and amounts to judgment.

Spending time observing nature can help reduce the mind's tendency to label and judge. When you look at a man-made object, like a building, it's easy for your mind to assign labels and form judgments. You might notice if a building is dirty, needs painting, or is decorated in a style you dislike, which can trigger critical thoughts. If you see a very attractive building, your mind might respond positively, making you wish you could live or work there. In contrast, when you look at a cloud or a forest, there's less for your mind to critique. Clouds exist as they are, and forests stand in their natural state, making it harder for the mind to judge and label them. The same applies when you gaze at a fish in an aquarium or watch a cat clean itself—the mind has very little to say in these moments. You can appreciate their mystery and be in awe of them without needing to label and judge them.

A simple sparrow is full of mysteries that are beyond our comprehension, and how much truer is that for a person or the Divine? The mind tends to believe it has everything figured out, declaring, "This is how it works." However, true wisdom begins when you can say, "I don't know." The mind craves simple answers and fears uncertainty, but pretending to have all the answers is a delusion. Surrendering involves letting go of the need to understand everything and finding comfort in not knowing. When you embrace this state of acceptance, a deeper form of knowing begins to emerge. This deeper "knowing from unknowing" has been articulated by mystics throughout history, including Meister Eckhart and John of the Cross.[28]

There are many things we cannot know—but we do know that negative and repetitive thoughts can have a detrimental impact on our health and well-being. Unfortunately, if you are like most people, you have been taught very little about how to quiet the mind. I have been teaching children's Sunday school classes for twenty-five years and have volunteered as a tutor in the public school system for many years, yet I have never seen this topic addressed in any standard curriculum. This exclusion is unjustified and represents a failure in both our secular and religious education systems.

I've noticed that many churches discourage mental stillness out of fear of being perceived as "Eastern." Spiritual growth is often confined to the study of scripture, faith, obedience to the commandments, and the practice of sacraments. While these are all valuable, if you don't learn to gently take control of your thoughts and emotions, you will experience unnecessary suffering, as will your family, friends, and coworkers. You are responsible for your inner space, and only you can clean up the mess. It's good to seek counsel from others, but *only you* can do the inside work. Nobody else can do it for you or decide what's best for you.

Mental stillness is not a precarious or abnormal state of mind. The mind naturally becomes quiet when negative, unhelpful, and repetitive thoughts are subtracted. Mental stillness makes room for positive, constructive thoughts when needed and, more importantly, lets you experience the peace that transcends all understanding[29] beneath the mental noise. This kind of peace has nothing to do with the mind or its thoughts, which is why it is said to transcend understanding.

---

28. Dupre & Wiseman, Light from Light, p 356
29. Phil 4:7

Inner peace, along with the joy and love that accompany it, is like a buried treasure. To uncover this treasure, you must dig through layers of dirt. The outermost layer may consist of physical pain, while deeper layers contain unwelcome thoughts and emotions. To work through and subtract these layers, you need to engage in introspection—an inward examination of your feelings and other bodily sensations. In the next chapter, we will explore how to shift your focus from your mind to your body, allowing you to release both emotional and physical pain.

Chapter 14

GET OUT OF YOUR HEAD
AND INTO YOUR BODY

Emotions are defined as mental reactions that are typically accompanied by physiological or behavioral changes in the body.[30] The renowned neuroscientist Candace Pert was among the first to assert that the mind and body are *not* separate. Pert viewed emotions not just as mental events, but as physical processes involving the release and reception of neuropeptides located in the brain *and* throughout the body. She argued that the mind and body are deeply interconnected at a molecular level, and that the emotional sensations we experience in the body are the physical manifestations of our subconscious mind.[31]

A key characteristic of the subconscious mind is its inability to distinguish between reality and fiction, and it also lacks a sense of time.[32] As a result, our emotions can often be irrational and not aligned with the actual moment; therefore, they should not be taken too seriously. While feelings add richness to our lives, it is essential to remember that *feelings are not facts.*

Emotions—both pleasant and unpleasant—are meant to be experienced, not suppressed. Emotions are typically felt in the heart or the gut, but they can also be experienced throughout the torso, neck, face, and extremities. The range of feelings your body can produce is vast and nuanced. Consider the subtle differences in how your body responds to anger, anxiety, jealousy, guilt, agitation, regret, sadness, loneliness, depression, boredom, happiness, elation, ecstasy, and many others.

---

30. https://www.merriam-webster.com/dictionary/emotion retrieved 5/5/25
31. Candace Pert, Your Body is Your Subconscious Mind
32. Mapes, Imagine That, p.16

Different individuals may experience the same emotion in diverse ways or in various parts of their bodies. For instance, some people may experience anxiety as a rapid heartbeat and nausea, while others feel cold hands and feet, and some may notice a vague heaviness and tension. It's essential to identify and acknowledge your feelings so that you can give them the attention they deserve instead of suppressing them.

Paying attention to emotions doesn't mean you have to understand them—it simply means being aware of them. Some philosophies emphasize the importance of understanding your feelings, but emotions don't always make sense. There are times when understanding can help, but overanalyzing your feelings can make them worse because you're feeding them with thoughts. *Emotions are constantly changing and shifting like the wind—if you leave them alone, they will pass.* Your main task is to be aware of your feelings and let them pass through you freely as they arise.

Emotions enrich our lives much like a musical soundtrack enhances a movie. However, unlike a carefully crafted soundtrack, our emotions do not always align with the situation at hand. Soundtracks are intentionally designed to match scenes, and without music, films would feel dull and lifeless. Similarly, without emotions, our lives would lack vibrancy and depth; however, emotions can sometimes conflict with reality. For example, you might be safe and comfortable lying in bed, yet feel a sense of anxiety as if you were in danger. Alternatively, you may find yourself at a fun and lively party, but your emotions might convey a dark and somber tone, leaving you puzzled about why this is the case. Due to this disconnect, it's essential to remember that we cannot always trust our emotions.

Putting trust in your emotions is called "emotional reasoning," which happens when a person uses their emotions to draw false conclusions about a situation or themselves, and their feelings are held as proof that something is true. Examples of this are as follows:

- *"I feel jealous, so my partner must be cheating on me."*
- *"I feel uneasy, so something terrible is about to happen."*
- *"I feel scared, so I know I'm going to fail."*

- *"I feel lonely; therefore, I must be unlovable."*
- *"This investment feels right, so I'm putting all my savings in."*

Emotional reasoning can lead to false beliefs that seem right but are entirely erroneous. The reality is that feelings are not facts, so if you trust and follow them, you may get lost.

Emotions can be very persuasive, much like a confident used car salesman trying to sell you a lemon. As we discussed earlier, simply saying, *"Isn't that interesting?"* can help you distance yourself from your emotions and become a silent observer. In addition to that, when you become aware that your feelings are attempting to lead you to believe something false, you can say out loud, *"Feelings are NOT facts."* Together, these two statements serve as a gentle "one-two punch" to the false self.

Feelings and thoughts form a two-way street: thoughts trigger feelings, and feelings can trigger thoughts. For instance, when you think an angry thought, your body tenses up, preparing you for a fight. On the other hand, feelings can precede thoughts, such as when you encounter a bear in the woods. Initially, you feel fear, followed by your mind generating fearful stories.

Thoughts and feelings often go hand in hand, but that's not always the case. Some thoughts, like "Should I have pancakes or waffles for breakfast?" are neutral and lack an emotional component. Conversely, some feelings may arise without any accompanying thoughts, such as waking up in a bad mood for no apparent reason. However, bad moods don't remain free of thoughts for long. Your mind will start crafting stories to explain the mood. As these stories develop, a cycle begins between your mind and body.

The cycle of thoughts-to-feelings and feelings-to-thoughts is a feedback loop like a microphone placed near a loudspeaker. The loudspeaker produces sound, and the microphone amplifies it, sending the sound back to the speaker, which in turn sends it back to the microphone, and then to the loudspeaker, creating an endless cycle that produces an annoying screeching noise. Thoughts and feelings can create similar mental and emotional noise that is self-sustaining.

You break this cycle by paying attention to the feelings in your body instead of feeding the thoughts in your head. The more attention you give to your feelings, the less attention remains for the thinking mind, causing the cycle to come to an end. Unpleasant feelings should be welcomed just like pleasant ones, so that you are not resisting the feelings and attaching mental stories to them.

When you experience a strong emotion, it can trigger reactions that might lead you to say or do something you'll regret later. Your brilliant mind knows what to do when combined with awareness, but it may not work properly if overwhelmed by emotional energy. That's why it's essential to first pay attention to the sensations in your body and release some of that energy before trying to use your mind. Taking a few deep breaths and spending a few seconds in silence can often create the space needed for awareness, leading to clearer and more focused thinking.

The intelligence within your body is truly remarkable. Your body knows how to digest food, fight infections, regulate temperature and blood pressure, heal wounds, eliminate toxins, and perform countless other complex tasks of which you may be unaware. The sensations your body produces play an essential role in this intelligence. Although we're often taught that there are only five senses—sight, hearing, smell, taste, and touch—the human body can generate over thirty different sensations, and these can be experienced in various combinations.

The sensations in your body serve as signals for your attention and should not be ignored. For example, if you sprain your ankle, you need to pay attention to the pain to help the ankle heal. Ignoring this can cause a minor sprain to worsen into a serious problem. The early stages of illness often cause fatigue, which serves as a warning to rest, allowing your body to combat the sickness. If you ignore this and push through your usual activities, you may become more ill and take longer to recover. When you're in a dangerous situation, the sensations of fear alert you to react quickly by fleeing or taking other immediate actions; ignoring this could be life-threatening. Notice how moments of real danger temporarily quiet the mind, creating a state of presence, awareness, and alertness.

Your body can also respond to more subtle dangers, such as changes in your environment. For instance, when you travel to an unfamiliar location, you may notice that your digestive system slows down, leading to constipation for a few days. This reaction is not something you consciously choose; it occurs automatically due to the low-level stress from the new surroundings.

Whenever you experience constipation or other changes in your digestion, it's a good opportunity for self-reflection. Consider that you might be resisting something or worried about something that is contributing to your stress. A more extreme example of this is Irritable Bowel Syndrome (IBS), which can involve both constipation and diarrhea. Studies indicate that a large percentage of IBS patients also experience generalized anxiety disorder and depression—this connection is not coincidental.

Additionally, twitching eyelids and facial muscles may indicate that something going on in your life is not to your liking, suggesting that it's time to practice surrender. Remember, surrender is not about making everything okay—it's about being okay with everything.

Not all the sensations produced by your body are intelligent. The sensations of anxiety are often irrational, and many people experience anxiety attacks for no obvious reason; however, they should still be given attention. Unfortunately, we often ignore these bodily sensations—such as heaviness, tension, a rapid heartbeat, and nausea—and instead return to our thoughts, which leads to more suffering, much like the feedback loop between the microphone and the loudspeaker. The sensations of anxiety should be viewed as a call for your attention—*even when they do not correspond with real danger*. Attention, that is, as the silent observer, without mental commentary. If you practice paying attention to anxious feelings each time they arise, they will gradually pass through you, no matter what the cause—more about anxiety in the next chapter.

Many people believe their attention can be in two places at once, a phenomenon known as multitasking, but that is not true. Many studies have shown that attention can quickly switch between tasks, creating the illusion that it is in two places at once, when in fact it is not.[33] This is why focusing your attention on the feelings in your body pulls attention away from your mind, and it is why most meditation techniques include conscious breathing or paying attention to other bodily sensations to quiet the mind.

My experience with chronic pain—such as lower back pain—is that it is my body's way of trying to help me, and perhaps trying a little too hard by drawing my attention to physical pain instead of emotions such as anger and anxiety. My conscious mind is easily distracted by physical pain, so this causes unpleasant thoughts and feelings to stay contained in my subconscious. During my journey into chronic pain, I rarely thought about my anger or anxiety—I was mainly focused on the physical pain in my back, neck, elbows, hands, and elsewhere. The anger and anxiety were certainly there, but my body helped to suppress these feelings by keeping me focused elsewhere. I'm not suggesting that this process is necessarily helpful, or that it happens in everyone; it's simply the nature of the mind and body in some people.

Although it's difficult to determine exactly how this happens, two mechanisms have been proposed. The first, which I have observed in my own experience, involves amplifying and memorizing pain signals from past injuries or other minor structural issues. The second proposed mechanism suggests that the body induces pain by restricting blood flow to specific muscles, nerves, and tendons, leading to oxygen deprivation, inflammation, and physical pain. This would explain the burning sensations and numbness in my hands and feet during the most challenging part of my pain journey.

Stress-induced migraines clearly illustrate how physical pain can be a powerful distraction. While you can choose to ignore your emotions, a migraine is impossible to ignore. It forces you into a state of mental quiet and relaxation, whether you like it or not. This is why those who suffer from migraines often seek out quiet places to be alone. In my experience, even positive, constructive thinking during a migraine episode can create enough tension to escalate the pain. I've learned that the early stages of a migraine are a message from my body that says:

---

33. https://pmc.ncbi.nlm.nih.gov/articles/PMC8715974/ PMID: 34965913 retrieved 5/28/25

"Stop all thinking and relax." As soon as I sense this, I pause whatever I'm doing and quiet my mind, which usually helps to stop the escalation of the migraine.

It is not always convenient to pause and quiet my mind in stressful situations, and sometimes I wish I weren't prone to migraines or didn't have such a sensitive nervous system. However, these challenges have become my greatest teachers. Many people on the spiritual path have found that their greatest strengths lie within their weaknesses,[34] and this has certainly been true for me. These weaknesses have taught me valuable lessons that have helped me grow.

One of the most valuable lessons I've learned is that the surest way to remain stuck in pain is to suppress your emotions. The distracting power of physical pain supports your choice to suppress emotions, which is why pain becomes amplified, memorized, and can linger for years. When you suppress unpleasant feelings, you do not allow their energy to pass through you; instead, you store them so they can resurface later to trouble you further. As we've already discussed, humans have developed various techniques—including constant activity, excessive TV and phone use, obsessive involvement in hobbies and sports, being a workaholic, and positive thinking—to suppress uncomfortable thoughts and feelings.

On the other hand, many people believe that they must *express* their emotions to be free from them. However, the truth is that expressing your emotions does not necessarily eliminate or reduce them. Punching a wall when you're angry may feel good for a short time, but it will not release the anger. In fact, it can reinforce that anger instead. The same applies to raising your voice, swearing, throwing objects, or slamming doors. You might feel a momentary release as you expend some energy, but the source of that energy remains unchanged.

Most people assume there are only two options for dealing with emotions: suppressing them or expressing them. However, there is a third option—*pure experience.*[35] This means relaxing and attending to

34. 2 Co 12:9
35. Singer, Living Untethered, p 143

the emotion to experience its energy. The more attention you give to the emotion, the less attention remains to feed the thoughts in your head with another story. This breaks the continuous feedback loop that sustains the energy. If you can relax and lean into uncomfortable emotions without adding mental commentary, they will gradually pass through you rather than being stored.

Suppression and expression will keep you stuck in pain; however, once you become comfortable *experiencing* all your feelings, their energy will freely flow through you. Once you choose to experience all your emotions, there is no longer any need for the distracting power of physical pain, so it will gradually begin to resolve on its own.

But how can anyone truly relax and feel comfortable with an uncomfortable emotion? If you ride bicycles, horses, or ski, you understand the importance of wearing a helmet. In the long run, it helps prevent significant pain and suffering. While helmets can be itchy, sweaty, irritating, and distracting, you accept these minor inconveniences as part of the sport and choose not to resist them. Similarly, if you want to grow and fully experience life, you must accept and welcome the discomfort associated with certain emotions instead of fighting against them.

Facing deep emotional pain can be likened to jumping into a cold swimming pool when you don't want to go swimming. However, once you get past the initial shock, you can choose to stay in and acclimate to the water. You may not be happy about it, but you can accept the situation and let it be as it is. The moment you accept an unpleasant emotion, its grip on you will start to loosen. Embracing emotional pain is the key to freeing yourself from it. Remember—"the way out is the way in."

Each time you allow yourself to fully experience emotional pain, some of that pain will pass through you and be released for good. Every moment you stay with an unpleasant emotion—without adding another story—brings you one step closer to freedom. *However, while practicing this, you might feel worse before you feel better.* This is because a significant amount of emotional pain may have been stored away, ready to surface.

Remember that stored emotional pain is like magma beneath a volcano—it stays dormant until something in the outside world triggers it to erupt. This could be something someone says or something you see that brings the pain to the surface. When this happens, don't be discouraged. Instead, relax and allow the pain to rise and pass through you. Although reliving the pain may be difficult, remember that the discomfort is temporary. If you avoid attaching a narrative to the pain, it will eventually flow through you and be released.

In the first few chapters of this book, I discussed some triggers that caused past pain to resurface. When this pain emerged, it often felt overwhelming, leading to chronic physical pain because I didn't know how to relax and let it go. It's important to remember that minor irritations can be magnified when they trigger stored pain, meaning you might not always be upset for the reasons you think. If you notice that your reaction is disproportionate to the situation, it's a clue that this is happening. You don't need to understand why you're overreacting—the key is to relax into it, allow it to flow through you, and release it.

You must be vigilant and relax immediately when you feel an emotional disturbance. If you hesitate and allow your thoughts to take over, it will be much harder to re-center yourself. One minute of negative thinking can create enough momentum for your thoughts and emotions to drag you along with them, like the raging current of a wild river or a freight train with no brakes. Once this happens, they may need to run their course for a few hours before you can re-center yourself. Don't be discouraged by this—it is a natural part of growth and happens to everyone. Freedom does not come from trying to release deep emotional pain all at once; you won't be able to do this. Freedom comes through the practice of relaxing into the minor irritations you encounter every day.

There are times when I'm going about my business and feeling great, and then suddenly a wave of anxiety or depression hits me out of nowhere. In many cases, there isn't a prior thought or situation to trigger it. It's like a hungry monster that suddenly appears and demands to be fed with dark thoughts. When that happens, I immediately relax and gently refuse to feed it, and it usually leaves. I observe this brief drama within myself regularly, and it's actually become entertaining to the point where it often makes me smile. *I can smile knowing that it's not who I am.* The fact is, however, that the false self wants to be in charge—the wicked master—and can be very cunning and persistent. It will invent new ways to draw your attention to useless or toxic thoughts again and again. But if you relax and don't take the feelings seriously, they will leave you every time.

Shifting attention away from the mind and into the body isn't something you do occasionally. During a typical forty-minute rush hour commute, when many distractions try to bother me, I may shift my attention away from my mind and into my body twenty times or more. With practice, you'll learn to relax hundreds of times throughout each day as disturbances attempt to take hold of you.

Relaxing or leaning into unpleasant emotions can be a challenging concept to explain and practice, as we have become accustomed to ignoring feelings or trying to fix the situations we believe cause them. When I try to explain leaning into the body's unpleasant feelings, I often receive a lot of puzzled looks. Although not many people practice this, you can be one of the few who do.

I understand that when you're dealing with intense physical pain, like lower back pain, it's very difficult to attend to the emotions in your body. I've been there, and I know how tough it can be. During those times, the best approach is to pick up a pen and paper and spend a few minutes twice a day jotting down your thoughts and feelings. This simple form of mechanical meditation will calm your mind and broaden your awareness—helping your physical symptoms start to subside. Once your pain lessens, you can delve into the emotions within your body and discover a deeper sense of freedom.

Remember—inner peace, joy, and love are like buried treasures. You may need to dig through several layers of dirt to uncover them. One of the most challenging layers to dig through is anxiety, which we will explore next.

Chapter 15

FORTUNE TELLING (WORRY)

Fortune telling—also known as worry—is predicting that something terrible will happen in the future. The mind automatically generates stories about what might go wrong. Worry hijacks your brilliant imagination, turning your mind into a wicked master. Worry can consume you, making you feel like a different person, almost as if a foreign entity has taken possession of you. This feeling of possession results from identifying with these thoughts, which feed your false identity—the false self. Worry does not serve you in any way and is poisonous to your health and well-being. Learning how to let it go is critical, and anyone can learn to do that.

The terms worry and anxiety are often used interchangeably, but worry is more about thoughts, while anxiety relates more to bodily sensations. Worry and anxiety typically occur together, but that is not always the case. Anxiety attacks can happen without any conscious thought and may be a programmed response triggered by subconscious processes that you are not aware of. You can learn to release anxiety even if you do not recognize the thoughts behind it.

There are no limits to human imagination, making it capable of concocting endless dreadful stories about the future that seem believable. These stories and the feelings they evoke can be very convincing—especially if you've been taught to trust your emotions. However, feelings are not facts, and most of these stories are illusory and not grounded in reality. The voice in your head—the false self—does not know what it's talking about, and it cannot be trusted. *When a politician makes a promise about the future, you don't take it seriously—you must learn to apply the same skepticism to the worrisome voice in your head.*

The voice of worry is universal, and most people seem to accept it as normal. It is rarely viewed as an obstacle to spiritual growth or a moral issue, as nearly everyone worries. In the famous Sermon on the Mount,[36] however, it is condemned alongside anger, judgment, and greed, because it is equally toxic to your spiritual development. It's remarkable how many spiritual individuals who have let go of anger, judgment, greed, and other vices still grapple with worry. Even the elderly in their final years face struggles with worry and anxiety.

Some argue that worry is necessary for planning wisely for the future, but worry is not the same as effective planning. Worrisome thoughts emerge automatically, while planning is done willfully and represents a constructive use of the mind. Planning entails a brief and voluntary visit to the future with a precise intention, followed by an immediate return to the present.

Some have suggested that worry is a valuable survival tool that has helped humans stay alive by considering all possible dangers, such as marauding barbarians and saber-toothed tigers. While there may be some truth to this, in our relatively safe modern world, such thoughts can become a liability and may even make you sick.

You may notice that wild animals often seem skittish and nervous; this behavior is essential for their safety from predators. *Similarly, your animal instincts are focused on your survival—not on your happiness.* However, spiritual growth involves rising above these instincts and taking control of your thoughts and emotions.

You have been given a great gift—the freedom to choose. While worries about tomorrow do arise automatically, it is ultimately your decision how to respond to them.

There is a positive form of mild anxiety known as constructive tension. This occurs naturally in situations such as taking an exam or giving a speech. Constructive tension is a natural response that helps you stay focused in the present, rather than being a result of worrying about a negative future.

---

36. Mt, chapters 5-7

Predicting the future, apart from weather forecasting, is much like consulting a fortune teller at a local carnival. Many people consider visiting a fortune teller to be unwise. Nonetheless, they often engage in their own form of fortune-telling by imagining bleak scenarios about their future or that of their loved ones.

Likewise, while some may deem it foolish to watch horror movies, they often imagine horrific scenarios in their minds. You can't watch horror movies all the time and expect to feel okay. It's like drinking poison and then wondering why you feel sick. If you've ever seen a horror movie, you know how it affects your body: you might feel butterflies in your stomach, tightness in your chest, a rush of adrenaline, a faster heartbeat, and overall tension. Likewise, worrying about the future can trigger the same physical reactions, leading to unnecessary suffering.

We all have a subconscious part of our mind that constantly watches the thoughts and images we consciously play in our heads. The subconscious mind is particularly sensitive to emotionally charged images, does not perceive time, and cannot distinguish between reality and imagination.[37] Therefore, any frightening situations you imagine occurring in the future can trigger feelings of anxiety in your body, as if they are happening in the present moment.

With practice, you can intentionally create positive visualizations to replace automatic negative thoughts. By imagining positive events in the future, you can trick your subconscious into believing they are real, allowing you to use this to your advantage. Unlike automatic worries, positive visualizations are created consciously and can have a beneficial impact on your subconscious mind. Visualization, a form of positive thinking, is a valuable tool for preventing anxiety, especially when anticipating a challenging situation. However, I do not recommend using it to suppress your feelings once they arise.

The best way to manage anxiety without suppressing it is to focus on the physical sensations of anxiety in your body. These sensations should not be ignored or pushed away. Instead, use them to shift your

---

37. Mapes, Imagine That, p.16

attention away from your mind and its negative stories about the future. By paying attention to your anxious feelings, you create some space and become the observer of the anxiety. This helps you recognize the folly and absurdity of worry and see that it does not serve you in any way. If you can maintain this space for a while, the anxiety will slowly pass through you.

Remember to always work with your body *before* engaging your mind. If you try to use positive thinking, such as visualization, to manage anxious sensations—like heaviness, butterflies in your stomach, a racing heart, adrenaline rushes, or tension—you will only suppress these feelings. First, take some time to relax and release some of this energy. Once you've re-centered yourself, you can explore using visualization and other forms of positive thinking. *Always attend to the body first and the mind second.*

Despite the progress I've made, I still occasionally have anxiety attacks. Sometimes, I can identify the trigger, like an upcoming social event that makes me uneasy, but I'm not consciously worried about it. In these moments, my mind stays relatively calm, yet I still feel physical anxiety. Remember that worry and anxiety are different—worry involves thoughts, while anxiety manifests as physical sensations. For me, anxiety is a rapid, pounding heartbeat paired with a heavy sensation in my chest. I've learned to interpret this as my body's way of calling for attention. When these feelings arise, I find a quiet place to sit, relax, and focus on my heartbeat, welcoming the sensation instead of fighting it or wishing it would go away. Most of the time, the anxiety subsides within a few minutes. Knowing I have this escape has made these episodes less frequent, and when they do happen, I don't take them too seriously.

If you're feeling anxious right now, take a moment to identify where that anxiety is manifesting in *your* body—everyone is different. Allow those feelings to exist without trying to push them away. Instead of getting caught up in stories about the future, notice how you feel in this moment; then relax and welcome those feelings. If you're unsure *why* you're feeling anxious, approach those feelings in the same way. If you can do this for even ten seconds, you may find that the anxiety begins to lose its grip on you. The more you relax and embrace those feelings, the more their hold will loosen, much like the Chinese finger traps that become easier to escape from when you relax your hands.

To live completely free of worrisome thoughts—you must learn to surrender. As we've discussed, this means letting go of future outcomes and not insisting that life unfold in a specific way. When you are open to any outcome, your mind will run out of things to say, and you will be free of worry. It's natural to want life to go smoothly without any bumps in the road, but that is not reality. I encountered one of these bumps not too long ago.

I recently applied for life insurance, which required a medical exam as part of the application process. Shortly after the exam, I received a letter indicating that one of my blood test results was outside the normal range, prompting me to see a doctor. This particular blood test measures a cancer marker called CEA (Carcinoembryonic Antigen), which some life insurance companies require for underwriting purposes. An abnormal CEA level doesn't necessarily mean you have cancer; it merely suggests that there may be some cancer present.

My doctor ordered several imaging tests and a colonoscopy to investigate the possibility of cancer. I had to wait weeks for the tests to be performed, and during that time, my mind began to spiral with all sorts of worrisome thoughts about the potential cancer I might have. This caused significant anxiety and a feeling of being possessed by it. For quite some time, I did not feel like my usual self.

I practiced quieting my mind by jotting down my worrisome thoughts on paper. I mainly wrote during my daily quiet times, but I also took brief pauses throughout the day to jot down my thoughts and feelings. This practice helped me to begin observing my feelings of anxiety instead of identifying with them. Once I created some internal space, I no longer felt possessed by the anxiety.

Anxiety is both energetic and relentless—at times, I still felt it pressing on me as a heaviness in my gut. When that happened, I shifted my attention to this heaviness. I would sit in a chair and silently observe it for a few minutes, relaxing as much as possible. I practiced welcoming the uncomfortable feeling and did not try to push it away. This allowed most of the heaviness to pass through me and release.

A few days before my scheduled colonoscopy, I decided to intentionally visualize a favorable scenario to replace the worrisome thoughts that had been playing on repeat in my mind. I imagined the doctor approaching me in the recovery room after the procedure, wearing a big smile and telling me that everything went well and no problems were found. This wasn't an effort to change reality but a comforting image for my subconscious mind to hold onto. When the time finally arrived, I felt completely relaxed, and afterwards, the doctor told me that he didn't find anything concerning.

I eventually decided to surrender—which meant becoming indifferent to the outcome. If cancer were found, I would deal with it, and that would be that. My mind quieted once I became open to any possibility, and all my worries and anxiety disappeared. This wasn't easy—but it demonstrated the power of surrender and non-resistance to the flow of life.

In the following months, I underwent several imaging and blood tests, all while maintaining my acceptance of any possible outcome. This mindset allowed me to find peace most of the time. While this practice did not change my reality, it did silence the useless chatter in my head.

The CEA test was repeated months later and remained unchanged, which is a good sign. A year later, it was retested and was still unchanged. In the end, nothing was found, and I didn't waste more than a year worrying about nothing.

Surrendering to situations like these can involve the constructive use of your brilliant mind. For example, suppose you're worried about losing your job. Your company is not performing well, and rumors about layoffs are circulating, leaving you unable to shake off this fear. Use your mind constructively and ask yourself, "What is the worst that can happen?" Perhaps you will need to find a different job or collect unemployment benefits for a while. If your income is reduced, you may have to adjust your lifestyle. Use your mind constructively to consider all the various scenarios and see if you can be okay with the worst outcome. If you can accept it, you have surrendered and are free. Your mind has nothing more to say, and the automatic worrisome thoughts will stop.

You can also use your mind constructively to make a list of everything you've worried about since childhood. Take a moment to review how many of those worries actually came true. You'll probably find that most never happened. If one of your past worries did happen, think about whether you were able to handle it. Chances are, you managed it, or someone was there to help you through it—*because situations in the present are always manageable.* Even if they weren't easy or pleasant, you got through them and grew because of those experiences. Present challenges are relatively easy to handle compared to illusory thoughts about the future. Worries about the future are like steam rising from a kettle—you try to grasp the steam and do something with it, but there's nothing there.

You don't have to handle tomorrow, next week, or next year. The only thing you need to handle is what's happening right in front of you at this moment. Let your life unfold, and tackle challenges only when they become real. In other words, "*Take therefore no thought for the morrow: for the morrow shall take thought for the things of itself.*" [38]

My parents were both prone to worry, and my mom, in particular, had a long-standing fear of getting cancer. For at least forty years, this worry troubled her. If you consider that she worried about it for one hour each day—*that totals over 14,000 hours of unnecessary suffering.* Eventually, my mom *was* diagnosed with breast cancer later in life. Fortunately, she received treatment and made a full recovery. The entire process, including surgery and office visits, took about forty hours—far less than the countless hours she spent worrying.

Would you rather endure 14,000 hours of anxiety or just 40 hours dealing with the present reality? Dealing with reality is always preferable to worrying about it, even in the most challenging circumstances.

Worry is a natural part of our automatic programming, but you can start reprogramming yourself today. Visualization is an effective

---

38. Mt 6:34

way to achieve this, though it requires effort and practice. A simpler approach is to use affirmations. Affirmations are positive statements that you speak out loud with conviction, helping to reprogram the automatic thoughts generated by your subconscious mind.

Affirmations shouldn't be spoken just once—they should be repeated regularly, much like a commercial that plays on TV hundreds of times. When you say an affirmation, do so with the same conviction and enthusiasm that actors do in commercials. These commercials are designed to implant automatic thoughts that prompt you to buy products, and you can use the same technique to reprogram your mind positively. We will explore the concept of reprogramming in greater detail in Chapter 19. For now, whenever you feel the urge to worry, repeat the following affirmations out loud—and with conviction:

"My thoughts and feelings about the future are NOT facts."

"I deal with reality instead of worry."

"There are no refunds for time spent worrying."

You can create your own affirmations for specific situations by carefully choosing words that express a solution *in the present tense*. Avoid discussing past problems or projecting them into the future. Instead, focus on verbalizing the solution as if it is happening right now. For example, if you're worried about having a difficult conversation with your partner, you can say out loud: *"I'm having that talk."* Repeat this affirmation whenever the thought comes to mind—perhaps a hundred times or more. In a short time, you will find yourself having that conversation naturally, without fear or effort.

The mind often tries to solve worrisome problems in the middle of the night, which can keep you awake. However, very few problems are resolved during these late hours. If worry prevents you from sleeping and your mind refuses to let go of these thoughts, whisper this affirmation to help calm your mind: *"I'm not solving this puzzle now."* Each time your thoughts wander back to the problem, gently repeat this affirmation again and again. This affirmation can also be used throughout the day whenever your mind starts to fixate on a problem at an inappropriate time.

Affirmations empower your true self to gently take charge, instead of letting the mind be your master. I incorporate affirmations into my daily quiet time and find it helpful to write them down. Affirmations are powerful and can reprogram your mind, making automatic thoughts disappear completely.

There are situations in life where a big worry can hit you unexpectedly—like a tidal wave. In such cases, your best option is to sit with the feeling. Recently, my wife called me at work to say that our son, Ayden, was "dysregulating." He was becoming emotionally unhinged and violent, even throwing things at her. It was reminiscent of the Tasmanian Devil from the Bugs Bunny cartoons, whirling through our house and causing chaos. This wasn't the first time this had happened, but that day was Ayden's twenty-third birthday. He stood over six feet tall and weighed 225 pounds, making the situation quite serious. I instructed her to call 911 for assistance and rushed home, initially overwhelmed by a wave of fear.

With a forty-minute drive ahead, I had plenty of time to worry, and a dark, heavy feeling quickly settled over me. As I drove home, I chose to stay with my feelings and focused on the sensations in my body—knots in my stomach, tightness in my chest, tension in my face, and tears welling up in my eyes. By doing so, I began to calm my racing mind. Instead of dwelling on what my wife had told me, I chose to allow and notice the energy moving through my body.

By doing that, I was able to maintain some space inside and arrived home feeling relatively calm, focused, and prepared to deal with whatever came next. The police and an ambulance were there, and Ayden had mostly calmed down. Nobody was seriously injured, and only minor damage was done to the house. I did not change the situation, but I did change my response to it. By accepting my anxiety instead of feeding it with negative thoughts, I made myself available to be of service, and I grew a little in the process too.

Every moment of life—particularly the challenging ones—presents us with an opportunity for growth. Each moment holds great value because our time to experience life is limited. When we dwell on worry, we squander time that cannot be regained.

When you accept uncomfortable feelings like anxiety, you transform that emotional energy into a deeper awareness that leads to growth in your true self. This process is known as transmutation and helps you build your "presence power" instead of feeding your false self with unhelpful or harmful thoughts. This growth is permanent and will stay with you forever. The transmutation of negative emotions into "presence power" is like converting trash into clean electricity at a modern clean-energy power plant. Every bit of emotional trash can fuel your growth, allowing your light to shine brighter. However, if you suppress or ignore these feelings, they will eventually return to trouble you even more.

Worry can blind you to the bigger picture, so it's beneficial to regularly assess your life and perspective. At this moment, as you read this book, how many of the following boxes can you check off?

[ ] Are you safe from war, criminals, natural disasters, or other threats *right now*?

[ ] Do you have access to clean air, clean water, healthy food, and sanitation *right now*?

[ ] Are you warm, dry, and clean with a roof over your head *right now*?

If you can check all these boxes, you're doing better than most people on the planet. Maybe your mind is racing with worrisome thoughts, and you feel uneasy inside, but when you look at the big picture, you're doing pretty well right now. Why not accept and enjoy the moment that's happening right now?

There's a simple mental game you can play to help you let go of most worrisome thoughts. Pretend for a minute that you have only one month left to live, and then ask yourself if the things you're worried about still matter—the answer to this question will usually be no. Next, extend the timeframe to one year and ask the same question, and in most cases, the things you're worried about still won't matter. Continue pretending that your remaining time to live is five years, and then ten years, and then keep going until you reach a point where you realize it's not a game anymore—*your time really is limited*. When it comes to worrying, does it matter if you have one year left or thirty years left? The fleeting nature of life is a reality for everyone, and it makes no sense to throw away *any* of the time you have left to worry. Contemplating the brevity of life is a powerful spiritual practice that will help liberate you from worry, and we will explore this further in Chapter 24.

Chapter 16

ATTACHMENTS

An attachment is the mistaken belief that something or someone is necessary for experiencing peace, joy, or love. Attachments create emotional dependence on possessions, careers, and relationships, and our culture encourages us to identify with these elements. While these aspects of life can bring enjoyment while they last, they do not define your true identity and are ultimately transient.

Attachments can fool us into believing that we truly want certain things, but in reality, what we seek are the pleasant feelings they promise to produce. Soon after we get what we want, we often ask, "What's next?"—because the feelings we sought have faded away. No object, person, or career can bring lasting peace, joy, or love—these wonderful feelings come from within and cannot be found outside ourselves.

Attachments can be a significant source of anger and anxiety. You become angry when something stands in the way of the attachment you want. Conversely, the fear of losing an attachment can create anxiety. Attachments may have great surface appeal, but upon closer inspection, you'll find they harbor the seeds of pain and suffering.

Attachments feed your false identity by leading you to identify with things. Do you feel broken when your car breaks down? Do you feel down when your stocks and bonds are down? Do you feel lost when you lose your job? If any of these are true, you've identified with these things. Remember, spiritual growth involves subtraction, so you need to let go of these attachments if you want to grow. Letting go of attachments doesn't necessarily mean getting rid of these things—it means disidentifying from them.

It's natural for us to shape our identity around material possessions, careers, and relationships. We've been conditioned to believe that acquiring the right possessions and cultivating the right relationships will lead to lasting happiness. When we feel unhappy, we often think we need more or better things, a more fulfilling career, or improved relationships. In reality, our attachment to these external factors sows the seeds of unhappiness within us.

An attachment can lead to a form of fortune-telling in which a person predicts their future happiness by thinking, "I won't be happy until I have the thing I want or meet the right person." This mindset can prevent you from experiencing happiness in the present because it convinces you that true happiness exists only in the future, tied to specific possessions or relationships. This type of thinking also manifests as living for the next vacation, living for the weekend, or living for retirement. It's only logical that if you spend your life waiting for happiness to come in the future, you will never find it.

Lasting happiness that exists independently of future events is called inner joy or the joy of being—*this can only be found in the present moment.* Though it may be difficult to define, inner joy arises from a state of peace and contentment and embodies feelings of vibrancy and enthusiasm. I liken it to a calm, misty lake early in the morning—despite its stillness, the lake is full of vibrant life. To experience inner joy, you don't need to add anything to your life; instead, you need to remove the obstacles that block it.

Consider a new car that brings you happiness for a short time. However, think about how you feel when you get your first dent or scratch. At that moment, the seeds of suffering begin to sprout. While the dent or scratch can be easily fixed, you might feel as if something inside you has been damaged, which can ruin your day. In reality, it's your false identity that feels damaged—not just the car. If you are a perfectionist, you may think that the car is now no good; this is known as all-or-nothing thinking, which we'll explore later. When something happens to an item you're identified with, you take it personally. Your mind interprets it as a personal attack, and your emotions reinforce that belief. In contrast, when your neighbor's car gets a dent—it hardly affects you.

Many years ago, my mother lost the diamond from her wedding ring. Our entire family began searching for it by crawling around on our hands and knees for days, checking every nook and cranny of her house. Despite searching tirelessly, we couldn't find it. Mom was distraught and fell into a state of depression. The lost diamond held significant sentimental and material value, and there was no consoling her. Although I felt empathy for Mom, since it wasn't my diamond, I remained emotionally detached. Many days later, she found the diamond under a radiator in the corner of the living room, and everything was right again. I was concerned about finding the diamond, but my mother's attachment to it created a very different experience for her.

Attachments create a false sense of ownership because, in reality, no one truly owns anything—we enter this world with nothing and leave with nothing. What if you viewed your belongings as though they were merely on loan to you? What would it be like to take responsibility for the things entrusted to you while staying emotionally detached from them? Imagine the freedom that perspective could bring.

Your false identity—the false self—does not want you to have this freedom because that would lead to its demise. The false self wants you to identify with your stuff and build more and more attachments. The false self says, "This is my house, this is my car, this is my diamond. I need more, and nothing better go wrong with my stuff." Each attachment you add to your life strengthens the false self and creates bondage to material things.

Freedom from attachments comes through awareness. Awareness always sees the big picture, which includes one certain truth that everyone agrees on—Atheists, Christians, Jews, Muslims, Hindus, and Buddhists all agree that we're here for a short time and will leave all our stuff behind when we go. If this is a certainty, why not embrace it now instead of pretending it isn't true? Why waste even a moment of peace and joy by getting upset over stuff? You can enjoy stuff while you're here, but identifying with it will only lead to suffering.

The next time you notice a dent or scratch on your new car, furniture, or smartphone, take a moment to acknowledge your feelings about the situation and relax. Consider the bigger picture in life, and practice saying out loud—"This is a very small problem." Allow the situation to be as it is instead of wishing it were different—*this is what surrender means.* Surrender doesn't imply inaction; it means taking the right action without a reaction. In this case, that might involve scheduling an appointment to get the item repaired and then letting it go. Accept that the item may no longer be perfect. If you still feel bothered after it's been restored, try saying out loud, "I'm okay with it not being perfect."

Every instance of damage or loss to your car, house, or any other possession presents an opportunity for growth by letting it go. Viewing your belongings as if they are on loan to you is not about renunciation or pretending—*it's about facing reality.* The house you currently live in will eventually belong to someone else; the truth is that you are merely a tenant entrusted with its care and maintenance. Your car will eventually change hands and then turn to rust. The diamond you possess isn't yours forever; it will eventually belong to someone else. The precious diamond Mom lost and found is now kept in a safe, waiting for the next person to wear it. It is evident that one's life does not consist in the abundance of one's possessions.[39] Why not embrace this reality and detach from material possessions now?

If considering the fleeting nature of everything leaves you feeling discouraged or depressed, take a moment to look at the other side of the coin—*pain and suffering are also temporary and do not last.* This perspective can bring great comfort when you're overwhelmed by pain, hardship, or a dark mood. No matter how hopeless things seem, tomorrow is always a new day; as the saying goes—"*This too shall pass.*" If you take a moment to reflect, you'll realize that much of the anguish you've faced in your life lasted less than a day. Indeed—"*What a difference a day makes.*"

Careers are another common form of attachment. Career attachment occurs when a strong emotional bond forms with a person's job or workplace. This can show as loyalty, dedication, or even dependence on one's job for self-worth and identity. When meeting someone in the

---

39. Lu 12:15

US for the first time, it's common to ask, "What do you do?" but in many other parts of the world, this question is considered rude because it reduces a person's identity to something very superficial.

A significant portion of life is spent building a career, so it's natural to identify with it. This has some value because it promotes satisfaction and a strong work ethic. However, careers can end suddenly for reasons such as economic shifts, technological advancements, or disabilities. Attachment to a career can also blur the line between work and personal life, making it challenging to keep them separate. Therefore, it's wise to detach from this false sense of identity now to prevent potential suffering later. You can put your best effort into your work while knowing that your career does not define who you are, nor is it the source of lasting peace and happiness.

Similarly, relationships can turn into attachments that satisfy emotional needs. Relationships are a wonderful aspect of being human, providing rich opportunities for growth. While relationships should be viewed as opportunities to serve others and share love—this is not always the case. People often seek something from relationships that they feel is missing within themselves. Therefore, they mistakenly look to relationships to *acquire* love, joy, and peace, believing they can find these feelings outside themselves.

The phrase "I cannot live without you" does not express true love—it reveals a dependence on seeking love externally. It's essential to reflect on whether your life is an expression of love or merely a pursuit of it. If you have no love to share and are looking for it outside yourself, it's a sign that you need to do some inner work. When love flows from within, others will naturally be drawn to you—you won't need to go looking for it.

It's also common to form attachments to recreational activities—such as mountain climbing, horseback riding, motorcycling, car racing, skiing, and skydiving—that involve an element of risk or require intense focus. To lose focus and start thinking while doing these activities could mean serious injury or death. Even the false self recognizes this and stops bothering you during these brief moments. As stated earlier, many people crave these types of activities not only because they are fun but also because they provide a respite from mental noise. Unfortunately, however, this is a precarious peace that lasts only as long as the mental focus is required. Once everyday life resumes, the mind resumes its chatter.

Affirmations can be used to let go of all types of attachments. For example, if you identify with your car or house and become upset when something goes wrong, try saying out loud—"I am NOT this house" or "I am NOT this car." Likewise, if there is trouble at work that is causing you to feel upset, you could say out loud—in private of course—"I am NOT this job" or "This job is NOT who I am." Repeating these affirmations with conviction will help you disidentify from that attachment.

Many popular teachings promote the use of affirmations to get what you want, but often, getting what you want is not what's best. As I've said, spiritual growth is always about subtraction or removing obstacles that hold you back. So, if you use affirmations to acquire more things—which is addition—you're essentially planting more seeds of suffering, and that doesn't make sense. However, when you use affirmations to let go of attachments and clear obstacles to growth, you'll notice that your desires naturally begin to change.

When you let go of attachments, you can respond appropriately, instead of just reacting when things go wrong. For instance, if you disidentify with your job, the displeasure of your boss won't affect you as much—you'll still put forth your best effort and let it go at the end of the day. If you *lose* your job or career, while it may be disappointing, it won't mean the loss of your identity. Instead, you will take immediate steps to find a new one. Similarly, when you disidentify with your possessions, such as your house or car, you won't let a minor repair ruin your day—you'll take care of it and move on.

Possessions have the power to possess you—even if you try to detach from them. Consider how much time and energy you invest in caring for your stuff. Do you need four cars, a vacation home, and all their maintenance? How much happiness do they truly bring you? Possessions can limit your freedom, so consider simplifying your life by getting rid of some things. You may discover you are much happier with less to clean and maintain.

The idea that "less is more" is fundamental in most spiritual teachings. Fewer material possessions can lead to greater satisfaction and deeper engagement with life. The less time you spend acquiring and maintaining your belongings, the more you can dedicate to sharing your love and serving others.

Attachments can consume you and lead to neglecting everything else in life. You can be consumed by a relationship, a business, a sport, a house, or even a car. This is why it is said, *"For where your treasure is, there will your heart be also."*[40]

You can also become consumed by *comparing* your possessions, career, and relationships to those of others. In the next chapter, we will explore how we perceive life through a distorted lens known as a "mental filter." This filter constantly compares our belongings to those of others, evaluating their worth based on differences. This is a form of insanity and a recipe for perpetual discontent and suffering.

---

40. Mt 6:21

Chapter 17

MENTAL FILTERS

A mental filter lets certain information pass through your senses while blocking out everything else. Your unique past experiences shape these filters and form the views, opinions, and beliefs that contribute to your false identity. Since no two people have the same past experiences, no two individuals share the same mental filters. These filters operate on autopilot and are often outside your conscious awareness. They can distort your perception of reality because you only see what your filters allow you to see. However, by developing awareness, you can dissolve these mental filters and connect with reality more effectively.

Most people perceive life through a mental filter I call "the comparator." This comparator evaluates your life in relation to others, highlighting only the differences. For instance, you might feel happy about owning a beautiful mansion with an indoor pool—but your happiness would diminish if everyone else had a similar mansion. Similarly, if you experienced a car accident and ended up in a wheelchair—you would likely feel very upset. However, if everyone in the world were in a wheelchair, you might find it easier to accept your situation.

Why do we constantly compare ourselves to others? The reason is that the false self thrives on these comparisons and feeds on having more. Notice how you can sometimes feel diminished when something good happens to someone else, or when someone has more or knows more than you. This kind of thinking is irrational and will only lead to ongoing unhappiness.

A good strategy for dissolving "the comparator" and expanding awareness is to write out a list of all the positive aspects of your life, regardless of what others have or do not have. Mental filters often favor the negative and obscure the positive, so writing out this list will help highlight the good that you cannot see. Make a habit of reading through the list during your daily quiet time or whenever you feel discontented with your current situation. As you review the list, take a moment to express gratitude for each item.

I recently put this idea into practice when my family moved to a new home to downsize, simplify our lives, and reduce the maintenance I had to deal with. Although it was the right decision, I was troubled that I didn't have a nice view of the woods, unlike some of my neighbors. My mind began to fixate on this and a few other negative things, causing me to feel increasingly unhappy. I could hear a voice in my head saying, "This house is no good, and I shouldn't have moved here."

One morning, I decided to take action. I grabbed a pen and paper and listed everything I liked about the house. Then, I made a second list of things I didn't like. Surprisingly, my "good list" had twenty items, while the "not-so-good list" only had three. I realized that my mental filter was blocking out twenty positive things and only letting in three negative ones. Next, I read through my "good list" a few times and expressed gratitude for each item. The negative voice in my head was silenced once I brought this filter into the light of awareness.

I have learned to make gratitude a habit by noticing the positive aspects around me wherever I go and expressing my thanks throughout the day. Cultivating an "attitude of gratitude" can transform your life because it diminishes the influence of the false self. Remember that the false self is that inner voice that continually points out everything wrong with the present moment. If you are a perfectionist, this voice can be especially loud, constantly criticizing what isn't ideal. Gratitude weakens this negative voice and clears away the mental filter, allowing you to see reality more clearly.

Another mental filter that obscures your view of reality is your belief system. You hold beliefs about a wide range of topics—politics, religion, healthcare, diet, nutrition, fitness, finance, relationships, and child-rearing. While beliefs are necessary for navigating the world, they can also blind you to what is real. Therefore, it's essential to be aware of your beliefs and to remain open to the possibility that there may be perspectives you haven't considered.

Many of your beliefs will change throughout your life, and some can shift from one day to the next or even from one moment to the next. However, the false self tends to cling to certain beliefs because they create a barrier to awareness, which can threaten to expose it.

When you strongly identify with a belief, you will feel the need to defend it fiercely when challenged. *Being right becomes a matter of survival because your very identity is at stake—being proven wrong can feel like losing part of oneself.* However, once you separate your identity from your beliefs, the disagreements of others will no longer affect you as much. You may still value your belief and recognize its importance, but you won't feel the same urgent need to prove anyone else wrong.

We all have belief systems, but not all of our beliefs are genuinely our own. Many beliefs have been instilled in us by others—parents, advertisers, the media, politicians, and religious leaders. *Anthony de Mello taught that one way to determine if a belief is yours is to notice whether you have a strong emotional reaction when it is challenged.*[41] A strong emotional response can indicate that a belief has been imposed on you by someone else rather than being one you hold independently. These externally influenced beliefs are often not examined. It is crucial to regularly assess your beliefs, especially those shaped by others. If you neglect this, life's realities may eventually challenge your beliefs—*forcing* you to question them. Engaging in a daily quiet time (see Chapter 9) and learning how to be a silent observer (see Chapter 10) will help you examine beliefs implanted in you by others.

Unfortunately, this is one reason why some religious institutions discourage meditation. As you learn to quiet your mind and observe your thoughts, a space will form between you and those thoughts. This space enables you to examine your beliefs—which are just thoughts—without identifying with them. This disidentification may lead to the dissolution of beliefs implanted in you by others as they are exposed to

---

41. Anthony De Mello, Awareness, p 27

the light of awareness. Once a belief that has been programmed in you dissolves, you can begin to think more critically.

Critical thinking is the process of analyzing, evaluating, and making reasoned judgments based on information. In today's world, this is increasingly vital because of the persuasive power of clever advertising and the media that constantly bombard us. However, our mental filters can greatly obstruct critical thinking, making it hard to see things clearly.

A helpful exercise to uncover your blind spots is to read books and articles by authors with differing opinions and worldviews. Many people avoid this because it's natural to seek confirmation of our beliefs rather than facing challenges to them. This happens because the false self fears "not knowing" and always wants to be right. If you engage in this practice, pay attention to any strong emotional reactions that arise when one of your beliefs is challenged. *If you react strongly, consider the possibility that this belief was given to you rather than developed by you.* Take the time to carefully examine it and decide whether to keep it or let it go. If you do choose to hold onto the belief, ask yourself if you have identified with it—would losing this belief threaten your sense of identity? Ultimately, all beliefs are mental constructs that do not define your true essence.

One type of short-term belief that everyone experiences is known as confirmation bias. This refers to a person's tendency to seek out, interpret, and process information that aligns with their preconceived notions and personal experiences while ignoring contradictory information. Large groups establish a standard or paradigm when they share similar and persistent beliefs. Letting go of widely held views and thought patterns is known as a paradigm shift.

Confirmation bias and paradigms can prevent you from seeing the facts right in front of you, no matter how open-minded you think you are. This often leads to a significant waste of time and energy and can sometimes result in serious mistakes. Therefore, taking breaks from incessant thinking is crucial, as we have previously discussed. These breaks can expand your awareness and help you recognize your blind spots. Thinking requires considerable effort and can create tension, so it's essential to balance it with the awareness gained through relaxation. If you practice a daily quiet time, it will become a natural habit to pause your mind periodically between thinking sessions, which will help reduce confirmation bias.

I sometimes experience confirmation bias when tackling technical problems as an engineer. For instance, a colleague once brought me a new product that wasn't working properly. Having faced a similar problem before, I was confident I knew the cause and how to fix it. I began taking measurements to confirm my initial assumption, but the results went against it. Still, I continued to look for evidence to support my belief, disregarding any conflicting data. Ultimately, I realized that my initial understanding of the problem was wrong. The real issue was a missing part that should have been obvious, but my preconceived notions blinded me to what was right in front of me—leading to a lot of wasted time and energy.

Your blindness is not the only issue at play. It's essential to acknowledge that others have mental filters that influence what *they* perceive and understand. You cannot convince anyone to believe something that does not align with their mental filters—*they will not process a single word you say*. Mental filters tend to favor the negative and overlook the positive. For instance, the Communist cannot see anything good in Capitalism, and the Capitalist cannot see anything good in Communism. Similarly, a vegetarian may not see anything good in a carnivorous diet, while a carnivore may not recognize the benefits of a vegetarian diet. When looking through the lens of your mental filter, you can only perceive the negative aspects of opposing views because the rest is filtered out.

Certain words can trigger mental filters—one such word is "God." When you hear it, your mental filter activates, allowing you to see and hear only what aligns with your beliefs about God. While it's possible to thoughtfully disagree with someone else's beliefs or opinions, these mental filters can make that difficult. If you don't believe in God or have a strong aversion to religion, you will perceive very little. Anything that doesn't fit your concept of "God" gets filtered out. For this reason, I prefer the term "The Divine," as it triggers fewer mental filters.

Mental filters are one reason spiritual truths are often conveyed through parables and poems rather than more familiar language. This principle is clearly expressed in the Gospels—"*Therefore speak I to them in parables; because seeing they see not, and hearing they hear not, neither do they understand*"[42]

Everyday conversations provide excellent opportunities to become aware of your mental filters and let go of the false self's need to be right—doing so can transform your relationships. Instead of striving to prove your point in your next conversation, focus on listening. Pay attention to what the other person is saying, and refrain from thinking about your next response. Quiet your mind, maintain eye contact, and observe and listen. Only share your opinion if specifically asked to do so. In business contexts, you may be expected to provide your opinion; however, this expectation is less common in personal situations. *Most people just want you to listen.* If you are being asked for your opinion on a personal matter, avoid telling the other person what they should do; instead, ask questions encouraging them to reflect.

There is nothing wrong with having periods of silence in a conversation—you don't need to respond immediately. Some of the wisest people I know pause for a few seconds before replying because they are genuinely listening to what the other person is saying. They begin to formulate their response only after the speaker has finished. Short pauses can also help reduce the reactivity of the false self. If you feel uncomfortable with the silence, use phrases like "Hmm, that's interesting" or "Hmm, let me consider that for a moment" to acknowledge the pause intentionally.

If you are asked for your opinion and there is a potential for disagreement, allow the other person to be right on some minor point. *Everyone wants to feel right according to their mental filters, so let them have that.* Avoid using the words "but" and "however," as they can imply that they're wrong and you're right. Instead, substitute the word "and." This slight shift can enhance any conversation and help prevent unnecessary arguments and conflict. Here are a few tension-reducing

---

42. Mt 13:13 ASV

statements that use "and" while allowing the other person to feel validated.

- "Your idea has some merit, *and* I would add…"
- "I understand your point, *and* suggest…"
- "That's a fair argument, *and* it reminds me …"
- "I see what you mean, *and* I recommend considering…"
- "There is some truth in that, *and* I think we need to discuss it further…"
- "I appreciate your insights, *and* that leads me to another thought…"
- "That's worth considering, *and* we should meet with others…"
- "Thanks for bringing that up, *and* I think it deserves review…"
- "That's a thoughtful idea *and* worthy of consideration."

Consider this conversation between my wife and me about where to go on vacation. She said, "We need to go to Disney World because it's a magical place and the kids need that experience." My perspective on Disney World was that it's very expensive, and the main experience involves waiting in long lines. Our individual viewpoints shaped our perceptions of Disney World in very different ways—I couldn't see the magic she saw, and she couldn't see the high costs and long lines I saw. This difference created significant potential for tension and disagreement.

As she spoke, I wanted to formulate a response to shut down the conversation and prove her wrong—instead, I listened quietly. After a long pause, I said, "*You're right*—Disney World is a magical place, *and* we should include it on our list of vacation options." Then I gently offered some of my vacation ideas. Initially, she reacted in a way that suggested she wanted to be right, but I continued to acknowledge her viewpoint using "*and*" statements from the list above. Ultimately, we reached a mutually agreeable decision without any argument. This listening approach, along with allowing others to be right, can dissolve tension and enrich all your relationships. *Who will argue with you when you tell them they are right?*

If you seek true freedom, choose to engage in real life instead of the filtered version created by your mind and its comparisons, opinions, beliefs, and need to be right. This means building your presence power—being present and aware—instead of allowing these thoughts to control your life. In the next chapter, we will delve more deeply into how mental filters formed by the past distort our view of reality and shape our false identity.

Chapter 18

THE PAST

Many people enjoy collecting things, but not all collections are worth keeping. I have a collection of arrowheads and stone tools that I've found in New England and other places. I enjoy examining my collection occasionally and imagining the rough hands of the Native Americans who shaped these stones into tools. However, our collections aren't limited to physical items—we also accumulate distressing memories and emotional energy from the past. Each time we revisit and relive the past, we replenish the energy in the collection, keeping it alive. This process distorts our perception of reality and can trigger automatic thoughts of past pain, self-doubt, resentment, guilt, and more.

When a farmer plows a field, he must focus on the plow. If he looks back over his shoulder, he will create crooked furrows and ruin the field. This principle underlies the saying: *"No man, having put his hand to the plough, and looking back, is fit for the kingdom of God."*[43]

Your life will become a similar mess if you constantly look back at the past. All of reality unfolds in the present, so to truly experience the fullness of life, your attention must stay in the now. Experiencing the present moment is indeed wonderful, but we often fail to appreciate it because the past influences our perceptions of it.

Many people find joy in the present moment—often without realizing it—by traveling to new places. This type of travel can be particularly enjoyable, as it exposes us to new experiences without past expectations to spoil the moment. Engaging with the unfamiliar can

---

43. Lu 9:62

evoke a childlike sense of wonder, temporarily quieting the mind until it inevitably returns to its usual habits of labeling and judging things.

I once had a friend who never planned his vacations and rarely visited the same place twice. On one occasion, I asked him where he was going, and he replied, "North." Next, I asked if he had any hotel reservations, and he said, "Nope." He reasoned that expectations often lead to disappointment, so why create expectations that inevitably result in disappointment?

It is natural to cling to memories that provide comfort and a sense of security, but this will only lead to greater disappointment. For instance, you might often replay a perfect vacation from ten years ago whenever you're feeling down. This memory becomes a source of cheer, and you may recall it countless times. Your positive thoughts about that vacation become deeply ingrained, forming a mental filter through which you assess all future vacations. Consequently, you may feel disappointment and discontent with any new vacation that doesn't measure up to the idealized experience you perceive through the lens of the past.

A similar situation occurs when you visit a new restaurant for the first time. If the food is exceptional and you have a great time, it's natural to reflect on that experience and set expectations for your next visit. However, upon returning for a second time, the experience may not feel as enjoyable, which can lead to disappointment. Even if the food and atmosphere are just as good as they were the first time, your prior expectations can distort your perception of the present. This phenomenon often makes new restaurants very popular for a while, until familiar expectations set in and they begin to feel like all the others. This is one reason why it is said that "familiarity breeds contempt."

This discussion isn't just about travel and dining; it also highlights how expectations can negatively impact your work. Consider how you feel when your boss compliments you. It feels great, and you replay that moment in your mind countless times. Consequently, you anticipate that your next boss will offer similar praise. If he or she fails to do so, you might regard them as a lousy boss. Furthermore, if your next boss is more critical, your negative reactions will be intensified because you've conditioned yourself to expect compliments.

To fully enjoy life and avoid adverse reactions, it's essential not to dwell on pleasant experiences from the past. While the mind wants to replay enjoyable moments, this can hinder your ability to fully appreciate what is happening in the present. Instead of clinging to memories, savor them in the moment as they occur, then let them pass through you. You don't need to try to forget them—just stop playing the reruns over and over in your head. Why allow the past to cloud your enjoyment of the present?

Unexpected moments often bring joy because they come without prior expectations. My wife and I recently returned from a highly anticipated seven-night Mediterranean cruise, during which we explored many magnificent sights in Rome and across Europe. We had a great time—however, this morning, I sat on the porch with my dog, savoring a cup of coffee while watching the sunrise and enjoying a warm, gentle breeze. This simple, unplanned moment brought me more pleasure than all the sights of Rome combined. Consider the joy you experience from these simple, unexpected moments:

- That beautiful sunset or rainbow that catches your eye.
- That small act of kindness or smile from a stranger.
- Your favorite song plays on the radio.
- Your dog puts his head on your lap and rolls his eyes at yours.
- An unfamiliar bird perches on your window and chirps sweet sounds.
- That perfect cup of coffee or tea exactly how you like it.
- The boss telling you to take the afternoon off

No amount of money can buy an experience as rewarding as these simple, unexpected moments. If you pay attention, you'll discover beautiful little things happening all around you all the time.

The best way to avoid disappointment and unmet expectations is to stop relying on the external world for happiness and instead look inward. When joy comes from within, you can appreciate all of life's surprises, both the highs and the lows. No matter where you are or what you're doing, always keep some attention inward, especially when you notice disappointment arising in your mind. Inner joy comes from a wellspring inside you that will never run dry or let you down.

I spent many years videotaping every family vacation, birthday, and holiday. However, one day I realized that I was experiencing only a small portion of reality through the camera lens and missing out on other vital aspects of those moments. I've learned to set the camera aside more often and be present instead. Relying too heavily on a camera can reflect a desire to cling to the past.

These were happy occasions, but the same can be said for distressing memories. While we can learn valuable lessons from the past, holding onto past pain does not benefit us or anyone else. Whether you have experienced something upsetting or have been traumatized by a terrible event, clinging to that pain comes at a high cost and provides no benefit.

Painful events from the past can program reactions in you that lead to self-doubt. If you are involved in the performing arts, you may struggle in front of an audience because of an embarrassing mistake you once made. If you're a figure skater, you may find it difficult to execute a particular jump because of a previous fall. An automatic voice in your head—the false self—reminds you of past failures, saying, "You're going to fall again," or "You're going to forget your lines again," or "You can't do this."

Conventional wisdom says that overcoming self-doubt involves mastering your skills and believing in yourself. Although this advice is valid, there is a deeper approach—*observing your thoughts and emotions allows you to liberate yourself from their control and no longer feel tethered to them.* When you disidentify from the voice in your head, you stop taking it seriously. When the voice of self-doubt says, "You're going to fall," you can smile and confidently say out loud, "That's not who I am."

Fighting the voice of self-doubt only reinforces its power, making it stronger. Freedom comes from acknowledging it and welcoming it in the moment it occurs. Once you relax and welcome it, a space will form, and it will lose its grip on you. Remember that the automatic voice in your head does not speak any truth—*it is mostly useless and irrational noise that should not be taken seriously.*

I sometimes experience the voice of self-doubt when riding dirt bikes and mountain bikes on the challenging rocky terrain of New England. Each time I encounter a difficult obstacle where I once fell, the automatic voice says, "You're going to fall again, just like you did last time." Identifying with this voice can lead to my falling, so I've learned to disidentify with it and become the observer. I do this first by *welcoming* the voice, then I say out loud—"That's not who I am." This statement helps separate me from the voice, preventing it from controlling me, allowing me to ride through the obstacle with ease.

You can also use visualization to reprogram self-doubt if you know of the situation beforehand. Many professional athletes utilize visualization to overcome self-doubt. Whether you're performing in the arts, engaging in sports, or delivering a business presentation, visualize yourself succeeding in advance. Avoid imagining a cheering audience or winning a prize—just focus on the actual performance. Envision the details of your performance setting, including the environment, sounds, and physical sensations. See yourself executing your task flawlessly, accompanied by the feelings of confidence and success that come with it. If you repeat this practice regularly for several days leading up to the event, your subconscious mind will accept it as reality, and the automatic voice will be silenced. Consequently, you *will* perform at your best without the false self holding you back.

Performing at your best requires learning to accept criticism. Past negative experiences can influence how you respond to constructive feedback. For example, suppose you faced public humiliation for a mistake in elementary school. In that case, you might feel uncomfortable and insecure whenever you receive criticism, even if it is meant to help you improve. When you find yourself struggling with criticism, take a moment to locate the uncomfortable feeling in your body and allow yourself to experience it, instead of pushing it away—this is non-resistance. You don't need to fully understand why criticism bothers you; all you need to do is relax and accept the emotional response it triggers in the present. If you can accept or even welcome this reaction without creating a mental narrative around it, the past will hold less power over you. This process can be challenging, especially if you've had traumatic experiences, but freedom begins with practicing with the minor emotional disturbances that happen each day.

Learning to *provide* constructive criticism, whether at home or at work, is essential for fostering growth in others. When offering criticism, it's important to avoid triggering unnecessary reactions or causing hurt. While people may appear tough on the outside, many are more sensitive than they seem. *Always focus on criticizing ideas and actions rather than individuals.* Targeting a person directly will only make them defensive and reactive. Instead, direct your criticism toward the idea or action—*never the individual.* For example:

- Instead of saying "You're wrong," try saying "I think the idea of_____ is not the best approach."

- Instead of saying "You need to do better," try saying "I suggest we do this differently."

The previous chapter discussed how "but" and "however" can evoke defensiveness. By swapping these words with "and," you can encourage a more positive conversation. Think about how you'd feel being on the receiving end of these two statements:

- I like what you've done, **but** I think it needs improvement…

- I like what you've done, **and** I have some suggestions to make it even better…

Which of them is more likely to trigger a negative reaction? Which is more likely to be helpful and encouraging? Take some time to practice a few "and" statements from the last chapter so that you will be ready to use them when the occasion arises. However, don't expect others to do the same for you—they likely won't. This practice is essential in relationships to prevent the accumulation of hard feelings and grudges.

Holding a grudge is like drinking poison and expecting someone else to die. The anger of unforgiveness can drag you down to a very dark place. Chronic physical pain often has its roots in the deep anger of unforgiveness. Chronic pain specialist Dr. David Hanscom explains that when his patients fail to make progress, it is usually their anger that holds them back because our anger and pain circuits are closely intertwined.[44]

The way out of pain often involves the path of forgiveness. Forgiveness is fundamentally about you—*not the person who wronged you.* Regardless of whether you have experienced betrayal, cheating, rejection, abuse, or abandonment, you bear the responsibility for the anger you are holding inside. *You* don't need to carry the burden of that person with you for the rest of your life.

Forgiveness begins with awareness of how you are affecting yourself, and refraining from feeding your anger with your "grievance story" or "victim story." Each time you revisit this story in your mind or share it with others, you are essentially taking a sip of poison and adding to your collection of past pain. Instead, practice being comfortable with the feeling of anger without revisiting the story that triggered it. This may involve sitting quietly for a few minutes each day, simply allowing yourself to be present with that feeling. It's not easy, but you must confront the feeling to be free from it. If you can sit with this feeling for a while, it will lose its power over you, and you will experience genuine forgiveness—not just the intellectual kind.

Your mind cannot forgive—only *you* can do that. Your feelings of anger, hatred, and resentment about the past will always seem justified and rational as you replay the stories in your head. The false self wants to prove that it is *right* and that everyone else is *wrong.* Your brilliant mind can find ways to justify or rationalize almost any thought, feeling, or behavior. Your capacity for self-justification is unlimited, meaning you can create a lifetime of unnecessary suffering for yourself.

Guilt resembles unforgiveness, but it is directed at yourself rather than at others. It is a feeling rooted in past actions you took, or failed to take, and it can linger for years, becoming overwhelming. Nobody is perfect—we all make poor choices, and the past cannot be changed, nor can words be taken back. The appropriate response to past mistakes is healthy remorse.

---

44. Hanscom, Back in Control, p 203

Healthy remorse involves a willingness to change, a desire to make amends, and an understanding of how our words and actions impact others. Healthy remorse occurs in the present—while guilt stems from dwelling on the past. Fixation on the past can lead to self-condemnation, feelings of unworthiness, and an excessive or misplaced sense of responsibility. The false self uses guilt to construct its distorted identity, so it is essential to learn how to release these feelings.

Letting go of guilt is similar to letting go of unforgiveness, which means no longer feeding it with your "guilt story" and becoming comfortable with the feeling until it loses its hold on you. Like all forms of forgiveness, this isn't easy—you may need to practice sitting with this feeling regularly and for an extended time to let it go.

When you decide to let go of the past, you may initially feel worse as you relax and lean into your collection of past pain. However, letting go of the past does not mean reliving every painful emotion from your collection one by one. Old feelings can be shed in large chunks rather than one at a time, allowing this process to occur quickly for some. Allowing yourself to experience past pain is not pleasant—it will hurt—but remember that pain and suffering are not the same. Suffering arises from the mind and the constant replaying of stories about the past and future. If you can quiet your mind while the emotional pain passes through you, it will hurt, but you won't suffer.

In most situations, letting go of the past involves inner work rather than outward actions. However, there may be times when you need to take specific steps. For example, you might need to reconcile with an old friend or repay a debt. If possible, it's best to address these matters immediately. If you can't, plan what you will do when the opportunity arises, and then allow yourself to let it go.

I am not a psychotherapist, but I recognize there is some value in understanding your past to comprehend why you react the way you do. However, it's essential to acknowledge that you cannot change the past, and untangling it entirely is often impossible. Understanding the past may be helpful—but to truly be free of it, you must practice letting it go as it manifests as automatic thoughts and feelings in the present.

When you allow yourself to experience past pain, that emotional trash will transform into "presence power," which enables you to tap into the energy of enthusiasm. Once this happens, instead of resisting difficult situations, you will have the energy and motivation to face them head-on. Enthusiasm is contagious and marked by lightness, clarity, and humor. The more emotional trash you process, the more energy you can transform, leading to greater enthusiasm.

Letting go of the past is essential for growth. You cannot pick up any book on spiritual growth, personal growth, or psychosomatic pain without encountering the concept of letting go of the past. This concept is crucial because past pain can run very deep and create extreme mental filters that completely distort the way you view the world. *Always remember that holding onto this trash brings no benefit and incurs a significant cost.* Decide right now that you will let it all go and burn it up.

Chapter 19

REPROGRAMMING

In the first chapter of this book, I shared my experience of moving when I was ten years old and starting fifth grade at a new school. This transition was very difficult, leading to the development of an automatic pattern of migraine headaches that followed me through college and beyond. As we've discussed, the most effective way to manage automatic thoughts and feelings is to learn to be comfortable with them, instead of trying to fight against them. The more at ease you become with these feelings, the less power they will have, and the less often they will occur. Additionally, you can take proactive steps to reprogram yourself to prevent these reactions from happening in the first place.

It is widely estimated that ninety-five percent of your automatic thoughts and feelings originate from the subconscious mind, which operates on autopilot and is not directly under your control. Your past experiences have programmed this part of your mind, and these programs are often outside your awareness. The subconscious is most easily programmed during childhood, but it can be reprogrammed at any point in your life with some effort. Many of the programs you are currently running are outdated and no longer serve you—they can even cause you harm. You can think of them as outdated software or malware on your computer that causes it to run inefficiently.

If you are skeptical about this, I encourage you to attend a demonstration by a skilled hypnotist. These demonstrations serve both educational and entertainment purposes, and can provide an enlightening experience. If you do attend one, you will leave with a new understanding of why you think and react the way you do. I've had the privilege of attending two such demonstrations by two different skilled hypnotists, one of which I discussed in Chapter 11.

During a more recent demonstration, I witnessed something unforgettable. The hypnotist selected a subject from the audience to receive a unique suggestion. Not everyone can be hypnotized quickly, so professional hypnotists use a variety of screening techniques along with their intuition to identify the most responsive individuals during demonstrations. In this instance, the demonstration began with a large group and gradually narrowed down to just one subject—a well-spoken adult female. After spending some time inducing a hypnotic trance, the hypnotist suggested to the subject that an invisible brick wall was blocking access to a part of the room. The location of this invisible wall was marked by a line drawn on the floor.

When the subject awoke from the trance, she had no conscious memory of the invisible brick wall suggestion. She was fully awake, alert, and speaking normally, but suddenly stopped when asked to walk across a line drawn on the floor. Confused about why she couldn't proceed, she began to blush. Despite being invited multiple times to cross the line, it was as though her feet were stuck in quicksand. She took a few steps back and tried to cross the line repeatedly, but she halted in her tracks each time. She smiled when asked what was wrong, saying, "I have no idea. I just can't go past this point. I don't understand this."

The rest of the audience and I were amazed by what we saw; however, bizarre as it sounds, the hypnotist didn't have any secret powers. He used the same techniques that advertisers, politicians, religious leaders, teachers, and even our parents use to influence our beliefs by programming our subconscious minds. This influence happens all the time—often without us realizing it.

We all carry past programming that we may not even be aware of, and letting it go is essential for spiritual growth. False beliefs ingrained in our minds can create significant obstacles, hindering our ability to perform even simple tasks, such as walking across a line on the floor. No amount of persuasion or reasoning will change this. In a hypnosis demonstration, these false beliefs are usually temporary and can be easily undone. However, beliefs formed in real life can last a lifetime.

This programming often happens unintentionally, arising from difficult experiences or the expectations and norms of our culture. One example of this programming is how *some* men refuse to seek medical attention even when they are seriously ill. Paramedics report instances where men experiencing a heart attack refuse to go to the hospital. This behavior has been programmed in them by societal expectations and gender roles. However, if you were to ask them to explain their reasoning, they would struggle to articulate it. They may logically understand that they should seek help, but they encounter an invisible barrier, much like the one faced in the hypnotic demonstration.

Another common example of subconscious programming is "white coat syndrome," where the presence of a doctor in a white coat automatically causes an increase in blood pressure. I used to experience this during my physical exams—my blood pressure would read sky-high in the doctor's office, and I would feel noticeably nervous. However, when measured at home, my blood pressure would be normal. The first time this happened was when I was in grade school. Being very shy, I had to be coerced into being a test subject for a blood pressure measurement in health class—which made me *very* nervous. I still remember the shock on the nurse's face when she saw the reading and the feeling of the entire class staring at me. This incident likely programmed and intensified my extreme case of "white coat syndrome".

If you pay attention to your reactions, you will notice that old programming can manifest in many situations. If you've had a negative experience with a particular doctor or hospital, you may feel anxious whenever you visit *any* medical facility. Similarly, if you felt overly pressured while buying a car from a specific dealership, you might experience dread whenever you enter *any* car dealership.

We've previously discussed the power of affirmations for reprogramming your mind to alleviate worry and attachments. You can use this same approach to break free from any old programming. Suppose you have an automatic reaction to medical facilities or car dealerships. In that case, you can create simple affirmations such as "Doctor's offices don't bother me," "I'm okay with hospitals," or "I'm fine with used car salesmen." When you notice these unsettling feelings, take a moment to relax and repeat your affirmation out loud with conviction. While doing this, allow the feelings to exist and do not suppress them. Over time, this practice will help eliminate the old programming in your mind.

Outdated programming can create barriers to accomplishing even the simplest tasks. For instance, someone might want to attend college but fail to submit applications, or an individual may have an expired driver's license yet not take the necessary steps to renew it. Each situation requires a simple action, yet progress is stalled because the person feels stuck. If you asked these individuals why they feel stuck, most would struggle to provide a rational explanation.

Affirmations can free you when you get stuck on small matters, like when I recently needed repairs on my house. For some unknown reason, I found myself procrastinating. It may have been because I didn't want to spend the money, or perhaps I was uncomfortable with having strangers in my home, or the repairs seemed too complicated to explain. Even though I didn't know the exact reason for my hesitation, I created a simple affirmation—"This repair is getting done."

I repeated this affirmation many times over a few days, and soon enough, I found myself typing a Google search for local contractors. One particular ad caught my attention, prompting me to call the number. A very polite gentleman answered and informed me that he was the owner of the business. To my surprise, he lived only a mile away and was actively seeking work, so he came over right away. The price was reasonable, and the repairs were completed quickly. After months of feeling stuck, a simple affirmation was all I needed to remove the obstacle—*even though I didn't understand the reason I was stuck.*

However, even if you know what's holding you back, an affirmation can help you overcome it. For example, suppose you need to ask your boss for time off but are hesitant because you fear he might react negatively. Come up with words that depict the conversation as happening. You might say out loud with conviction—"I'm having that conversation with the boss." Each time you feel stuck in fear, say those words out loud—like you mean it—even if you must whisper them. Soon, you will find yourself having the conversation effortlessly and without anxiety. You will likely look back and wonder why you thought it was difficult.

We often complicate our lives by holding onto false beliefs and fears, which limit the flow of grace into our lives. Grace constantly seeks to guide us toward growth and maturity, but we block this flow by allowing negative thoughts to accumulate in our minds, leaving us feeling stuck. When I use affirmations to reprogram my mind, I often notice unlikely circumstances—such as calling a nearby contractor who is seeking work—falling into place shortly afterward.

There is a remarkable passage in the New Testament that describes the power of affirmations spoken with conviction and their connection to prayer and Divine grace:

"...whosoever shall say unto this mountain, 'Be thou removed, and be thou cast into the sea', and shall not doubt in his heart, but shall believe that those things which he saith shall come to pass; he shall have whatsoever he saith." [45]

Is this passage about psychology or spirituality? I would suggest that the two are inseparable and that this passage encompasses both. Affirmations go beyond mental reprogramming and open us to grace. When you speak with conviction to the obstacles—mountains—blocking the flow of grace, those barriers will be removed. Once they are gone, grace begins to flow, and remarkable events start to happen. In some cases, they are so remarkable and unlikely that they make the hairs on the back of my neck stand on end.

Unlikely events that are meaningful are referred to as synchronistic events. We often recognize synchronistic events when they are pleasant, but in my experience, they are not always so. Unpleasant experiences highlight the areas where we need to grow and improve within ourselves. For example, my unlikely experience with the CEA blood test (see Chapter 15) was a lesson in surrender I needed at that time. Although it was unpleasant, the enduring reward is a deep freedom from worry. The birth of my son with Chung-Jansen Syndrome was an improbable *and* difficult event—less than one in a million—but

---

45. Mk 11:23-24

I would not have grown the way I have or written this book without him.

There is a flow to life that will help you grow if you don't resist it. You cannot change this flow, and it's futile to try. However, what you *can* do is align yourself with the flow just as it is. The flow of life is ready and waiting for you at every moment, and it wants to be your teacher. You might feel stuck like a riverboat caught on a hidden boulder because you've run into some unseen obstacle, but once you free yourself, you will rejoin the river's flow. Your view of the river will shift when you're unstuck—but it's the same river—just seen from a different perspective. You may *think* the river has changed, but it is *you* who have changed.

Chapter 20

PERFECTIONISM

Perfectionism can be seen as a virtue, as reflected in the saying, "Anything worth doing is worth doing right." Perfectionists tend to be highly conscientious and often achieve success in their fields. For instance, many successful engineers are perfectionists because people's lives are at stake when designing a bridge or a spaceship, so the details must be precisely correct. However, it can be taken to extremes in other aspects of life.

Perfectionism exists at various levels and can range from minor to extreme. Extreme perfectionism is resistance to life and will eventually lead to suffering. I used to embody extreme perfectionism, which undoubtedly contributed to my physical pain. Extreme perfectionists believe that if one part of a situation is flawed, then everything about it is wrong; this is known as all-or-nothing thinking. They adhere to a strict mental model of how things should be, which often conflicts with reality. The gap between their expectations and the actual situation equals the degree of suffering they experience. Extreme perfectionists can turn small situations into big disasters, blowing minor issues out of proportion into seemingly impossible barriers. They create problems in their minds that go beyond the reality of the situation. Perfectionists tend to be hard on themselves and are especially vulnerable to mind-body symptoms.

One Saturday morning years ago, I decided to paint a room in my house. After the paint dried, I noticed an obvious drip in the middle of one wall—it was at eye level and I couldn't ignore it. This led to a flurry of negative thoughts about myself because I felt I had made a mess of the room. I viewed the entire paint job as a total failure. I even considered removing that section of drywall and repainting the whole room. I couldn't find peace with that paint drip lingering there, and my agitation grew as I pondered the hopeless situation. The more I tried to forget about it, the more it bothered me. The paint drip threatened to ruin my weekend as I fixated on this small mistake, unable to see the bigger picture beyond the turmoil in my mind.

While surrendering involves "letting go" and accepting—perfectionism demands that everything must be a certain way. For those who struggle with extreme perfectionism, surrendering can be particularly challenging. However, accepting a less-than-perfect situation, even for just a few seconds, can create enough space within you for your true self to gain perspective and see the bigger picture.

I'm embarrassed to admit that it took me a while to relax and accept my feelings during this painting incident. After much distress over the disastrous paint job, a constructive thought finally emerged—"Since it's at eye level, I can hang a picture there to cover that paint drip and let it go." In that moment, I felt liberated and was able to reclaim the weekend. Nowadays, when I notice perfectionism creeping in, I say these affirmations out loud and repeat them several times:

"It's okay if it's not perfect."

"My life does not have to be perfect".

"I don't have to be perfect."

Perfectionists are highly driven individuals who can be extremely hard on themselves. They impose arbitrary deadlines and scold themselves when tasks are not completed on time or when they fail to meet their own standards of perfection. This negative self-talk often occurs silently, but I used to chastise myself out loud when I was alone. During the days when I was in the depths of intense physical pain, I frequently berated myself for trivial mistakes, such as misplacing a tool while working in my garage. I used words I would never direct at another person—yet, for some reason, I felt it was okay to use them on myself.

One day, I realized that I would never talk to a friend or child the way I spoke to myself. I was okay with calling myself an idiot, but I would never use that kind of language with any of my boys. So, I began to catch myself and change my self-talk. For instance, if I misplaced a tool, I would tell myself—"It's okay, I'll find it, just relax." Much like affirmations, gentle and positive self-talk can be transformative and should be expressed out loud whenever possible.

Negative self-talk often includes harsh labels, such as calling oneself a screw-up, unlovable, a failure, a loser, or a nobody. These labels are toxic and only reinforce the pain from your past. Start paying attention to the labels you use for yourself and consider how they would affect a child if directed at them. Asking this question can increase your awareness—and, in turn, help you be kinder to yourself.

Perfectionists often judge those who do not meet their standards, labeling them as idiots, fools, or worse. When you label someone, you engage in extreme over-generalization without taking the time to truly understand that person—who's probably not very different from you. This is often the case because we tend to criticize others for issues that we struggle with ourselves.[46] As you become more aware, you will start to see life through others' eyes and recognize the beauty and uniqueness of each person.

Even if you don't see yourself as a perfectionist, you still have a mental model of how the world *should* be. When you use "should" statements, it reflects a conflict between your personal standards and reality, leading to feelings of frustration and dissatisfaction. There are three types of "should" statements—your beliefs about how the world should be, your expectations of what others should say or do, and your thoughts about what you should be doing but aren't currently doing.

"Should" statements impose rules on how the world ought to operate that don't reflect reality. For example, if you drive on public roads, you will encounter bad drivers who create dangerous situations for others, and you might say:

"They *should* not drive like that."

"They *should* be more considerate."

"There *should* be more cops around when you need them."

---

46. Mt 7:3-5

As long as humans continue to drive cars on public roads, bad drivers will always be a reality. You cannot change that, so why let it bother you? As long as you live on this planet, you will encounter rude, inconsiderate, selfish, and thoughtless people. Why let that bother you? Nobody has the power to bother you unless you allow them—only *you* have the power to bother you.

"Should" statements often come with reactive energies that can lead to trouble. While anger might motivate you to say or do something appropriate, it's crucial not to react until you've re-centered yourself by taking some time to separate yourself from your anger. As we've already discussed, merely ten seconds of quietly observing the reaction in your body is often sufficient to re-center yourself. Once you are re-centered, you'll know what to say and do.

It's natural to want to tell others what they should do or how they should act, but this approach will only lead to suffering. As we saw earlier, the reality is that very few people want to be told what they should do, especially when it comes to personal relationships. *Most people don't want advice—they just want to be heard.* Telling others what they should do can be interpreted as judgment or manipulation. Healthy relationships are characterized by empathy and trust; however, this bond is delicate and needs to be carefully protected. Using should statements can harm relationships and drive people away.

One of the best ways to help someone is not by telling them what they should do, but by asking them to explain their problem to you. You may not be an expert on the subject, but encouraging someone to articulate their problem can help them expand their awareness, making the solution more apparent.

I remember grappling with a technical problem during my first job as a young engineer. My boss noticed that I was struggling and came over to offer his assistance. Although he didn't know anything about the issue, he asked me to explain the problem to him. I was initially reluctant, but as I started to explain, the solution became clear within a minute. He didn't say a single word—he just listened attentively. By encouraging me to articulate my thoughts, he helped me reframe the issue and gain clarity on it. I've since seen this scenario play out countless times.

When you see someone struggling with a problem, ask them to explain it to you. Verbalizing thoughts can be similar to expressive writing—it increases awareness and helps a person emotionally distance themselves from the situation. If *you're* facing a problem, try to find someone who will listen while you explain it. Personally, when I hit a roadblock, I often sit down and explain my problem to my dog—he is always eager to listen and give me his full attention.

"Should" statements directed toward oneself are often used to justify harmful behavior or show resistance to one's feelings or resistance to reality. Here are some examples that highlight areas where you may need to work on yourself.

- I *should* exercise (translation: I don't exercise)
- I *should* eat healthy (translation: I don't eat healthy)
- I *should* get that roof leak fixed (translation: I'm stuck and don't know why)
- I *should* not feel this way (translation: I'm resisting my feelings)

If you find yourself stuck in any of these areas, create a simple affirmation that expresses the change you want to make in the present. Start repeating this affirmation each time you catch yourself using a "should" statement, and say it out loud with conviction.

"Should" statements express resistance to accepting reality, and resistance is how the mind turns situations into problems. Mind-made problems go beyond the reality of the situation and cause unnecessary suffering. However, when you disidentify from the mind and stop resisting life's flow, there are no mind-made problems—only situations to manage or accept as they are. Situations themselves do not cause suffering; instead, it is the mind that transforms situations into problems through resistance, leading to suffering.

The universe contains at least two trillion galaxies, each with around 100 billion stars, and most of these stars have planets orbiting them. While we cannot observe planets outside our solar system, those we can observe have no problems. The only place where problems exist (so far) is here on Earth—where billions of minds operate. Outside of Earth, everything simply exists as it is—there are no problems. This may seem obvious or even trivial, but reflecting on this fact can be profoundly enlightening.

Recently, there has been a great deal of excitement and romanticism surrounding the prospect of sending people to Mars, with the possibility of this happening within the next twenty years. This enthusiasm is somewhat surprising, considering that Mars is completely barren and inhospitable, and presents risks that could make the journey a one-way trip. While there are valid scientific reasons to explore Mars, I suspect that one part of its romantic appeal is that it has no mind-made problems. People rarely talk about the problems on Mars because there are no minds there yet to create them; there are only the challenges of the mission. However, this will likely change once humans arrive and face the harsh realities. We *will* face new challenges that will test our brilliant minds, but unfortunately, we may also use our minds to resist, complain, assign blame, resent, regret, and judge Mars as good or bad.

When you learn to disidentify from your mind, you transcend the problems it creates, and it becomes a powerful tool for managing challenging situations. When you drop all resistance to life, you stop insisting that things should be a certain way, and perfectionism and "should" statements dissolve. Instead, situations that can be changed are dealt with, and those that cannot are accepted. This shift allows life to become an exciting adventure rather than an unending series of problems.

Chapter 21

MIND-READING

When you imagine what someone else is thinking about you—even though they aren't actually thinking of you—you are engaging in mind-reading. This habit comes from the false self, which relies on other people's opinions and perceptions to define itself. Mind-reading reveals how much you care about how others perceive your appearance, mannerisms, possessions, and lifestyle. The false self seeks approval from others, trying to inflate its image like a balloon. But this inflated image will eventually pop, causing suffering. As you become more aware and the false self diminishes, you'll care less about others' opinions. When you stop caring what others think, you can relax and stop wasting energy playing roles expected by others.

A trip to the supermarket can be an opportunity to observe the tendency to engage in mind-reading and to reflect on how much we care about others' opinions. In Chapter 5, I mentioned that Saturday morning shopping with my son often led to increased stress because I was concerned about how others perceived his behavior and my parenting skills. Mind-reading can generate a flood of useless mental noise. Consider the following examples of the mental chatter you might encounter during an ordinary shopping trip:

There's my new neighbor whom I met yesterday. What was his name? I've already forgotten it. I'm such an airhead; I need to avoid him so he doesn't think I'm a flake. Why is everyone looking at me funny? They can probably tell I haven't showered, or they're annoyed with my squeaky cart. There's Sam from church. He's going to see the beer in my cart and think less of me. Hmmm, that store clerk was awfully nice to me and complimented me—she could probably tell I was a mess and was trying to make me feel better.

You may experience similar mental chatter when traveling alone for business and dining at a restaurant by yourself.

I'm the only one here eating alone. Everyone else is part of a couple or with their family. They must think I'm a loser. They probably think something is wrong with me. They must think I'm unlovable. I'm going to wolf down my meal and get out of here as quickly as I can.

The truth is that no one in the supermarket is paying attention to you, and no one cares that you're dining alone at a restaurant. These mental illusions are fueling your false identity and generating mental noise, anxiety, and tension in your body.

Mind-reading can happen in relationships with people we know and care about, not just with strangers. For instance, if you text a friend and she doesn't respond for a day, you might think, "Maybe she's avoiding me because I did something to upset her." In reality, she may have lost her phone and never received your message.

If your boss walks by without saying hello, you might think, "I must have done something wrong, or I must be on the layoff list." However, the reality could be that he is preoccupied with a sick child at home and just didn't notice you.

Mind-reading can often lead to poor judgment in public situations. For example, if you see an elderly person fall in public, do you hesitate to help because others are watching? Are you worried about feeling awkward or being judged for making a mistake? Do you think someone else will step in to help, relieving you of the responsibility? In situations like this, respond appropriately to what is happening and ignore the voice in your head.

Another variation of mind-reading is known as "discounting the positive," which is often linked to perfectionism. When you discount the positive, you ignore or dismiss compliments. You may do this because you believe you could have done better or that anyone else could have achieved what you did. Nothing you do ever feels good enough to you, and you assume that others think the same. For example, in the supermarket dialogue above, the mind said: "…*that store clerk was awfully nice to me and complimented me—she could probably tell I was a mess and was trying to make me feel better."*

Ultimately, the conclusions you draw from mind-reading are based on false assumptions driven by fear and the desire to survive. Letting go of mind-reading and overthinking allows the true self to emerge, rather than the false self. From that place of authenticity, you can then make decisions rooted in love, courage, and kindness for yourself and those around you.

When you notice that you are engaging in mind-reading, view it as an opportunity for growth and a chance to dismantle your false self. Often, simply being aware of your mind-reading can help you stop it. If you find it difficult to avoid this habit, try shifting your focus to the physical sensations in your body instead of the thoughts in your head. In situations where you catch yourself mind-reading, you may experience tension or anxiety due to the belief that others are watching and judging you—even though they likely are not. This mistaken belief is a form of emotional reasoning, so it can be helpful to remind yourself out loud: "Feelings are NOT facts."

Letting go of the need to mind-read is a key step toward freeing yourself from the burden of others' opinions and judgments. When you stop caring about what others think, you are free to be yourself. *Being yourself—all the time—is a wonderful experience because it requires no effort.* Playing roles is hard work and demands a lot of energy. When you stop playing roles and embody authenticity, your fatigue, tension, and anxiety will decrease significantly.

You don't need to *think* about how to be yourself—you are your authentic self when you stop thinking. As you cultivate inner quiet, your false self will diminish, allowing your true self to flourish. Your true self is not interested in impressing others; its only desire is to serve others—this is true freedom.

Chapter 22

PRACTICE, PRACTICE, PRACTICE

My father spent his Saturdays working in the yard, and my brother and I were always called to help. As a result, dad would inevitably spend Saturday evenings lying on the floor, resting his sore body because he had a desk job and hardly moved during the week. I would suggest that dad go to the gym on weekdays to build up his strength so that Saturdays wouldn't be so overwhelming. However, he would point to the backyard and say, "That's my gym." His generation was unfamiliar with regular exercise because the generations before him had been more physically active due to their involvement in physical labor. But, like my dad, you will suffer on Saturdays if that's the only day you do physical work. The same principle applies to handling life's difficult situations—you will suffer if you wait until big trouble comes along and have not practiced daily with the small troubles. Practice always begins with easy things before progressing to more challenging ones.

Your daily practice consists of two parts—one that occurs in the comfort of your home or another quiet location (see Chapter 9), and the other is allowing life to be your teacher. As stated earlier, your daily quiet time at home is comparable to an athlete going to the gym to prepare for his sport, while letting life be your teacher is like an athlete competing in scrimmage games against a tough opponent.

Allowing life to be your teacher is like welcoming those pop quizzes given in high school that nobody likes, because life has a flow you cannot predict, and it won't always go the way you wish. Life will throw you punches, and you must roll with those punches. Rolling with the punches means doing what needs to be done and not reacting negatively. Each time you react negatively to a situation, you reinforce that reaction, making it more likely to be repeated. If you want to grow, you must practice responding to life without reacting to it.

When life presents a pop quiz, it's common to feel the urge to complain. However, complaining usually only serves to irritate those around you. If you can take action to improve a situation, there's no need to complain—just respond and make the necessary changes.

What follows are everyday situations you can use as opportunities for growth instead of problems to complain about. Not all of life's unexpected challenges come as a complete surprise. You can often anticipate which situations will trigger you, allowing you to prepare for them. By practicing how to handle familiar scenarios, you will better equip yourself to manage unexpected ones.

Pets

Dogs need to go outside, even when it's stormy, which can create challenges. I don't have a fenced yard, so when one of my dogs needs to do his business, I grab a leash and an umbrella and head out with him. When the dog is hit with a blast of wind and rain, he tenses up and refuses to go as usual, pacing around while we both get soaked. If I tell him to "hurry up," he picks up on my agitation and becomes even more tense. If there's a rumble of thunder, he panics, and then it's nearly impossible for him to go. We often go back inside—usually drenched and agitated—until he calms down, then try again. This process sometimes repeats several times.

A cascade of events like this can trigger a torrent of reactive energy in me that is difficult to separate from and can lead to agitation. This reactive energy can reach deep and trigger past pain that has nothing to do with the dog—remember, you are not always upset for the reasons you think. Next, I start noticing myself getting angry at my wife for insisting we have two dogs when I thought one was sufficient, and my mind will ask selfish questions such as, "Why isn't she out here dealing with this instead of me?"

When you're aware of potential scenarios like this that could disrupt your peace, you can avoid an adverse reaction and prevent adding to your collection of pain by anticipating the worst outcome before it happens. So, when it's storming outside and the dogs need to go, I've learned to embrace all the potential drama before I step outside. This includes getting wet, the dogs not cooperating, and making multiple trips. I gather some towels and open the dryer, preparing for the worst. When you are open to any outcome—instead of resisting it—your mind and emotions will have nothing to say, and there will be no agitation. These outings have since become comical on several occasions, and I've found myself laughing out loud in the rain.

That Difficult Neighbor

Many people, through no fault of their own, have a neighbor with whom they do not get along. This neighbor may be rude, messy, loud, eccentric, a troublemaker, or even a felon. Each time you pass by their house or apartment door, you may feel a subtle, automatic adverse reaction. This reaction often accompanies a narrative, leading your mind to add thoughts like—"I wish this person didn't live here," "I hope to avoid them," "I will never forget what they did," or "They're ruining the neighborhood." These programmed reactions stem from past experiences you've had with this individual, offering an opportunity for growth.

Next time you walk by your neighbor's door, allow yourself to relax into your discomfort without adding any mental commentary. Your mind may try to replay a past incident, but instead of doing that, focus on the sensation of discomfort. Take a moment to relax and breathe into it for ten seconds as you pass. If you regularly practice relaxing into this sensation, you'll notice that it decreases each time you walk by.

If you practice this daily for a few weeks, you may gradually shift from feeling negative to developing an awareness that enables you to see the world from your neighbor's perspective. You may begin to understand that their negative behavior stems from past experiences and does not define who they truly are at their core. The next time you encounter him or her, you may find yourself experiencing unexpected compassion or even love. While a busy mind tends to harbor disdain for difficult people—a quiet mind can reveal love.

If you pay attention to your body, you may notice that many places you pass regularly trigger negative feelings. For example, you might feel uneasy when you walk past a coworker's office with whom you had a bitter argument or when you drive by a car dealership that sold you a lemon. In these moments, relax and acknowledge the uncomfortable sensations without replaying the story in your mind. By practicing this consistently, you will allow these emotions to flow through you and gradually release. Ultimately, you will find forgiveness and release some of the pain you've been carrying.

Fatigue

Fatigue is neither an emotion nor physical pain, but it can trigger and amplify harmful thoughts and reactions in the same way. Most people find it more difficult to cope emotionally when they are tired, allowing minor issues to escalate into more significant problems. It's common to feel a slight sense of agitation in your body after a poor night's sleep. Unlike emotions, fatigue cannot be willfully released; however, you can learn to accept and become comfortable with it. I strongly encourage you to prioritize getting enough rest; however, if you feel fatigued and agitated, consider using it as an opportunity for growth.

Recently, a strong storm passed through town, keeping me awake for most of the night. As a result, I woke up feeling agitated and irritable. I dragged myself through my morning routine and faced heavy traffic on my way to work. Thoughts flooded my mind about how the day was going to be wasted and how I should have slept with earplugs. Instead of dwelling on those negative thoughts, I chose to shift my focus to the feeling of agitation in my body.

Next, as I drove, I played a game I call "Find the Feeling," where I try to locate the unpleasant sensations in my body. I noticed some agitation in my gut, some in my chest, and some in my neck and face. I spent a few minutes scanning these areas of discomfort and said out loud several times, "Isn't that interesting?" After this, I experienced a subtle shift. The agitation was still present, but I accepted it, and a space opened up inside me, allowing my mind to quiet down. While I was still driving, I focused just enough on these feelings to divert my attention from my thoughts.

Throughout the first half of the day, the stresses of work built up, and negative thoughts started to resurface—I was exhausted. Each time this happened, I paused to relax and focus on the sensations in my body without feeding them a story. I was persistent but gentle when shifting my attention back to my body. Eventually, the negative thoughts disappeared, and the day ended up being quite productive.

The thinking mind demands a great deal of energy, whether its thoughts are constructive or unconstructive. When you are fatigued, the mind lacks the fuel to operate at full throttle, so you can use this to your advantage and enter into a state of presence with less resistance from your mind. However, you must relax into the fatigue instead of fighting it; otherwise, the mind will find a way to keep racing. Each time you feel tired and irritable, treat it as a cue to relax and reconnect with your body. Fatigue can be transformed into "presence power," just like any unpleasant feeling.

Illness

The early stages of an illness can offer a valuable opportunity to connect with your body and improve your overall health. The body has remarkable intelligence that we often overlook. The immune system is part of this intelligence, and when it starts fighting an infection or any other threat, it signals for your conscious attention to help in the process.

During the early stages of a cold or flu, people often say, "I feel like I'm coming down with something." If you pay close attention to your body, you will notice a sense of "peaceful tiredness" before symptoms appear, or this feeling may accompany early symptoms. This feeling is very different from the irritability and fatigue caused by lack of sleep, and if you don't resist it, it can be quite pleasant and inviting.

I've learned to see this as an invitation from my body to give it my conscious attention. When I notice this feeling, I stop what I'm doing and find a quiet place to close my eyes and relax into the feeling for at least fifteen minutes. I do this while sitting upright in a chair to avoid falling asleep. I may repeat this a few times as long as the feeling persists. This can be very satisfying because it feels as if my body is asking for my attention, and I'm giving it what it wants.

In the past, I would resist this "peaceful tiredness" by grabbing another cup of coffee to boost my energy or taking a nap to sleep it off. While napping can be helpful, the mind can stay very active during sleep, which may not produce the same benefits as quieting the mind and consciously paying attention to the body.

This "peaceful tiredness" helps the mind calm down and disengage from constant thinking, allowing the body to conserve energy and support the immune system. During these moments, I've experienced beautiful states of deep relaxation that lead to creative insights. If you find meditation difficult, these low-energy periods can be valuable opportunities to relax, connect with your body, and achieve a quiet mind.

When I pay attention to and embrace these sensations, I often avoid getting sick altogether. Sometimes, I may develop mild symptoms, such as a slight cough or a runny nose, but these usually last only a day or two. I believe this is because I'm giving my body the rest it needs—which includes a quiet mind—and this seems to boost the immune system. If I ignore these feelings and push through with extra caffeine, I inevitably get sick. In my experience, the phase of "peaceful tiredness" usually lasts about half a day, so it's important to give it your full attention without delay. Once an illness takes hold, it may need to run its course. If this happens, you can still utilize the low-energy state of illness to practice quieting your mind.

Lines

As we've discussed before, the supermarket can be a great place to practice spiritual growth. I recently had the chance to put this into action while picking up some fresh deli cheese on my way home after a long and stressful day.

When I arrived at the deli counter, I felt relieved to see only one person ahead of me in line. I took a ticket but soon realized that this person had a very long list, and with only one employee working at the counter, my annoyance started to grow. I tried to remain positive, looking forward to relaxing at home with a cold beer, which offered some temporary relief; however, my frustration quickly returned. Though I was physically in the supermarket, my mind was elsewhere—lost in unproductive, repetitive thoughts.

I knew what I needed to do, so I focused on the irritation I felt in my body and began to relax. Instead of battling the irritation building inside me, I chose to experience the sensation fully. As I did this, my mind quieted, and I gradually became aware of the incredible place I was in. The deli was filled with a captivating array of smells from various meats, cheeses, and prepared foods. My ancestors, centuries ago, could never have imagined that such a place could exist. It struck me that most people on the planet would never have the chance to experience something like this, and yet here I was, upset about it. A sense of calm and peace washed over me as I stood in awe, waiting for my turn to be served, taking the time to notice my surroundings.

Remember that noticing is not the same as thinking. With practice, your true self can learn to notice all the information from your senses and the sensations in your body—whether pleasant or unpleasant—while remaining relaxed and aware. However, when you resist a situation instead of allowing it to be, noticing shifts into thinking, and you will suffer.

A similar approach to waiting in line can be applied at the checkout counter, DMV, bank, airport, or amusement park. A remarkable universe unfolds around you at every moment, no matter where you are. Incredible things happen even in the most ordinary situations, and you have the privilege of experiencing them all.

If you are standing in line outdoors, practice noticing your surroundings. Take note of the sun and how this incredible ball of fire never stops burning and never needs tending. Instead of thinking about the sun—just notice it. If it's hot and humid, notice how your body instinctively perspires when needed. Don't fight or resist the sweat; instead, relax and appreciate your body's remarkable cooling system. Feel the subtle movement of air across your damp forehead, even in the absence of a breeze. Acknowledge the pressure under your tired feet and the mysterious force of gravity keeping you grounded so you don't float away into space.

Your thoughts and emotions can block your awareness, preventing you from witnessing the miracle of life unfolding before you at every moment. Each time you find yourself waiting in line, practice noticing your surroundings—without thinking—and discover what you have been missing.

Car Trouble

Your brilliant mind can solve most problems when paired with awareness, as long as your emotions are not overwhelming you. However, many situations can trigger reactions that block awareness and constructive thinking.

For example, consider how you feel when you discover a flat tire on your car while you're rushing to work. Your mind can quickly spiral into negative thoughts, such as: "I'm going to be late for a meeting; I should have gotten new tires last week; I should have renewed my AAA membership; today of all days; this always happens to me," and so forth.

When you find yourself in a situation like this, take a moment to relax and focus on your body's reaction—just ten seconds can often break the cycle. This pause creates space for awareness, allowing your true self to find a solution. In this scenario, you might decide to call an Uber and fix the tire later. Many challenges in life have simple solutions, but we often overlook them because we react impulsively and let our false self take control.

The Weather

I enjoy camping and other outdoor activities, but camping in the rain can be quite unpleasant—if you resist it. I once read a story about a survivalist in the jungles of South America, where the rain was relentless. He said that fighting against the rain could drive you mad, as it can pour nonstop for up to ten days straight. To survive and keep your sanity, you need to accept the rain and embrace it as it comes.

I try to go camping when good weather is in the forecast, but New England summers often bring a chance of sudden thunderstorms, and it seems like I attract them. When it rains unexpectedly, my instinct is to resist and become angry. I remember one particular summer when it rained on every trip, which caused significant frustration and anxiety about future outings. However, resisting the rain isn't helpful and only leads to suffering, so why not welcome it instead?

When I go camping, I've learned to embrace the possibility of rain by planning for a complete washout and staying at a nice hotel to dry out if necessary. This constructive mindset enables me to accept any outcome, eliminating resistance to whatever happens. If it begins to rain, I relax and remind myself—and those with me—that we're on the only known planet where clean water falls effortlessly from the sky. I take a moment to appreciate the sound of raindrops hitting the tarp and the unique melody they create. When you don't resist the rain, it can be quite enjoyable to watch and experience. If things become too wet and uncomfortable, we head to a nice hotel with an indoor pool and a laundry room to dry out. This approach has transformed some rainy trips into fun adventures. This is an example of using constructive thinking to prepare for the worst possible outcome, instead of reacting negatively and resisting life as it unfolds.

The weather is ideal for learning non-resistance because it's obvious that you cannot control it. *The truth is that much of life is just like that— you believe you're in control, but you are not.* Numerous factors influence what happens every day, and very few of them involve you.

The following are tools and techniques to help you relax and prevent your false self from taking control. When you are in charge, your mind becomes a wonderful servant instead of a wicked master.

Don't forget to breathe!

During stressful situations, someone often says, "Take a deep breath and relax." Deep, regular breathing helps you relax, relieve tension, and increase your awareness. If you pay attention to your breathing, you may notice that it becomes shallow when you are tense. Shallow breathing can deprive your body of oxygen, leading to further problems and worsening the situation. So, when you encounter a stressful scenario, remember to breathe.

I often participate in organized off-road motorcycle events that involve navigating highly challenging terrain. The toughest sections are staffed with volunteers who assist and encourage riders who get stuck. Amid the noise of roaring engines, someone will inevitably shout, "Don't forget to breathe!" Experienced riders understand that when faced with difficult obstacles, the natural reaction is to tense up and hold their breath. This can lead to fatigue, serious mistakes, and even injuries.

Many situations in life can trigger similar reactions, where fear and self-doubt cause tension and shallow breathing. The root of the problem often lies within ourselves rather than in external circumstances. During these moments, breathing consciously and intentionally is essential to counteract the body's instinctive reaction to tense up.

Conscious breathing can be practiced any time and doesn't require your full attention. This technique is particularly helpful when you're engaged in a task and it's not practical to pause and quiet your mind. I sometimes find myself working under critical deadlines, during which I notice my breathing becoming shallow. When that happens, I continue working as the situation demands, and depending on how tense I feel, I may take several rapid and deep breaths—about two deep breaths per second for a minute or two—to help re-center myself.

When speaking in public, some individuals forget to breathe, making them sound awkward as they struggle to catch their breath. If you feel nervous while public speaking, take several deep breaths during the minute before it's your turn to speak. Before you begin, take a deep breath and exhale as you deliver your first sentence. This initial sentence should be short and memorized, such as, "Good afternoon, everyone, and thank you for being here." Aim to let this sentence flow out with one long exhale, and speak it louder than you might think is necessary. Doing this will dramatically improve the quality of your voice. Your audience will perceive you as relaxed and confident, reflecting that belief back to you. First impressions matter, so getting that opening sentence right is essential. Once you've delivered it, everything that follows will be much easier.

We've discussed counting breaths from one to ten during your daily quiet time at home, but this practice can be done anywhere, at any time. During a busy day, I sometimes find a quiet place, like a restroom, close my eyes, and count my breaths for a minute or two. During this time, I also check for any tension in my body and aim to relax a bit more with each breath. That brief escape from racing thoughts can help you reset and gain a fresh perspective.

Many excellent books are available on breathing and how to use your breath to promote relaxation and release emotional tension. The book *Breathing* by Andrew Weil, MD, was very helpful to me.

Look at the Sky

Observing the sky at different times of day can help quiet the mind and connect you with something deep inside. In New England, the sky often offers a marvelous display of clouds against a blue background, constantly shifting and moving. Clouds are both beautiful and vast, evoking feelings of awe and wonder, since each one is unique. The vastness of the sky and clouds can help put problems into perspective, making them seem smaller and less overwhelming.

Our minds tend to label and judge everything we see, but with clouds and the sky, there's not much to label, analyze, or criticize—they simply exist. One of my favorite retreats when my mind starts racing is to step outside and look up at the sky. This calms my mind almost immediately because there isn't much to say about clouds other than to enjoy their beauty and wonder. If I get distracted and start thinking about a man-made object that I like or dislike—such as a car or a house—I look back up at the sky, and my mind immediately quiets down.

A similar sense of awe and wonder can be experienced when observing mountains, sunsets, or vast, untouched landscapes. These feelings arise because the mind is briefly overwhelmed by their beauty, causing it to fall silent for a few moments. These inspiring feelings don't come from the sky or the mountains—they're just triggers that release something profound within you. Feelings of awe and wonder are always present and yearning to flow; however, they are often blocked by the clutter of your mind and its constant thoughts. As you learn to quiet your mind, this sense of awe and wonder will begin to emerge even with ordinary things. One day, you may find that a simple blade of grass or tiny ant can truly "blow your mind."

The Silent Commute

The next time you hop into your car and start your commute, turn off the radio and all other media, then proceed in silence for the first ten to fifteen minutes. Notice how uncomfortable the quiet makes you feel. Pay attention to all the unnecessary noise your mind creates and how it assigns labels to everything, forming judgments about other drivers and their cars. Notice how other drivers and situations can influence your thoughts and feelings, revealing that you are not always in control of your mind and emotions.

During the silence, focus your attention on the task of driving and observing your surroundings. Driving requires relatively little thought when your mind is not reacting. See if you can respond appropriately to what's in front of you without labeling, judging, or other mental commentary. Pay attention to the sound of the tires, the wind, and the engine. Be aware of the bumps and vibrations from different road surfaces, the steering wheel in your hands, and the pedals beneath your feet. Observe the horizon and the countless images whirling past you on either side.

Your mind will react to other drivers and various road situations. Each time this happens, take a moment to relax and refocus your attention on driving and observing your surroundings. This can be challenging, but aim to be quiet for ten seconds at a time. Your mind may tell you that you're wasting time and that it's boring. It might also suggest that you could be doing something more productive, such as listening to the news, a podcast, an audiobook, music, or making plans and phone calls. *However, the truth is that intentional periods of silence are never a waste of time—they are an investment in building your "presence power."*

When I started practicing silent commuting, a shift occurred in my perception. I began to notice things I had driven past a thousand times but had never been aware of. It felt as if I had put on a pair of wide-angle lenses instead of my regular glasses. I noticed landscapes, buildings, and trees as if they were new and had never existed before. This change in perception results from a quiet mind. When the mind is still, awareness expands like a floodlight—not a spotlight—allowing you to see what you were previously blind to. This wide-angle view will extend to all areas of life, not just the commute. You will start to gain new perspectives and insights throughout the day.

Periods of silent commuting serve as an excellent supplement to a daily quiet time at home, transforming the drudgery of commuting into an enriching and satisfying experience.

Mindfulness

The "silent commute" is an example of mindfulness, which involves giving everyday activities your full attention so the mind does not wander and get into mischief. Mindfulness keeps you focused on the present and prevents the mind from drifting into the past or the future. While mindfulness has become a popular term, it is a misnomer because it is about developing a quiet mind rather than a full mind.

You can practice mindfulness while doing something ordinary, such as unloading the dishwasher. The next time you do this, focus on the task instead of thinking about what comes next or rushing to finish. Try to relax and enjoy every aspect of the experience, rather than seeing it as a chore. Pay attention to each cup and dish, noticing how they feel in your hand as you pick them up. If there is any residual moisture, take the time to dry each item thoroughly before storing it away. Notice the smell coming from the dishwasher. Observe your feet as you carry each item to its designated spot. Pay attention to the movements of your hands, arms, and shoulders as you work. Listen to the sounds produced as you carefully place each item down. When you give your full attention to any task in this way, it becomes a genuinely satisfying experience.

Mindfulness can also be practiced at work and is especially helpful when performing mundane tasks you would rather avoid. For me, one of those tasks is boxing and shipping packages. Instead of resisting this task, I have learned to view it as an opportunity for growth. I pack each item carefully as if it were my most prized possession. I choose the appropriate box size and foam, meticulously tape every seam, and attach the label with care, taking my time and avoiding a rushed process. When you let go of inner resistance and accept an unpleasant task in this way, your false self diminishes, and your true self expands.

Mindfulness involves performing every task with great care and attention. The engineering lab where I work is equipped with many expensive pieces of equipment, each accompanied by a user's manual that explains how to operate and maintain it. Unfortunately, I have never come across a user's manual that instructs you to *care* about what you are doing—*caring is always paramount, but is often neglected.* When I have the opportunity to hire someone to work with me, I don't seek out the most intelligent or experienced candidate. Instead, I look for someone who cares about their work—ideally someone who loves what they do. If you care about your work, you will find a way to succeed, no matter what obstacles you face. Steve Jobs famously said, "The only way to do great work is to love what you do."

Body Scan

I include a body scan as part of my regular quiet time at home, but it can also be done anytime you find yourself sitting and waiting, such as in a doctor's or dentist's office. A body scan requires closing your eyes, so it's important to do it in a safe and preferably quiet space. Additionally, sit upright while performing the scan; if you lie down or recline, your body may interpret this as a signal that it's time for sleep, which is not the intended goal. The aim is to remain alert and relaxed while quieting the mind.

With your eyes closed, take a moment to relax each part of your body from head to toe, one at a time. Start by focusing on your left eyebrow and relaxing it for about five seconds. Next, shift your attention to your right eyebrow and do the same. Then, pay attention to each eyelid, relaxing them one at a time for about five seconds each.

Continue with your left cheek, right cheek, and lips, taking a moment to relax each one. Afterward, relax your jaw to ensure your teeth are unclenched. Then, move on to your ears and scalp, followed by the front and back of your neck.

Work your way down your body, relaxing your chest, shoulders, arms, hands, and each finger individually. Next, relax your belly, hips, thighs, calves, feet, and each toe one by one. Pay close attention to how each body part feels, focusing on releasing any tension that may be present. After completing your first pass, repeat the process to see if you can further relax each body part.

If you get distracted at any point, that's perfectly normal. Gently guide your attention back to the point where you left off. While doing this, your mind will produce automatic thoughts, but don't be discouraged. Focus on returning to where you were and keep relaxing each part of your body, one at a time. With regular practice, the noise in your head will gradually quiet down. Eventually, you'll find that you can do this even in the midst of background noise and activity.

Many people find stillness practices, including this one, to be very challenging. They often experience feelings of discomfort, awkwardness, and restlessness, especially if they are in physical pain. If you feel this way, take a moment to acknowledge your discomfort. Notice how your mind resists stillness and seeks to engage with thoughts, even if they are repetitive and unhelpful. If you find it difficult to remain quiet for more than a few seconds, that's completely okay. What matters is that you recognize your struggle with stillness, as this awareness is a vital part of the process. *Remember, there's no such thing as a bad quiet time—regardless of what happens, accept the experience and be at ease with it.* As stated earlier, if you are struggling with intense physical pain, going into your body will be difficult, and expressive writing is a better way to begin your practice.

The Mental Chalkboard

In the preface of this book, I describe a simple game I invented as a child that I still use to help me fall asleep. This game can also be played during the day, as long as it's safe to close your eyes for a few minutes. Refer to the preface for instructions on how to play. When played while lying down, it helps quiet your mind and prepare you for sleep. If you play it sitting upright, you will experience a sense of stillness and rest. However, keep in mind that this game may not work well for everyone, as it requires some ability to visualize thoughts.

Binaural Beats

Many individuals who struggle to achieve mental quiet often succeed by listening to binaural beat recordings. These recordings play two slightly different tones into each ear. The brain merges these sounds to create a third tone known as a binaural beat, which represents the difference between the two tones. This interaction results in the synchronization, or entrainment, of brainwave frequencies with the binaural beat frequency, helping to quiet the thinking mind.

Binaural beats are a modern technology that can effectively help you achieve a state of mental quiet in a short amount of time. It's best to listen to these recordings in a safe, quiet environment, and it's essential to wear headphones and close your eyes. Research has shown that specific binaural beat frequencies can enhance sleep, while others can induce relaxation and promote a sense of calm. Most recordings I have tried excel at quieting the mind, and I have noticed that the benefits extend beyond the duration of the listening session.

Various types of recordings are available to match your personal goals, typically featuring pleasant nature sounds that enhance the relaxation experience. You can find phone apps that play binaural beats, and while you can use earbuds instead of headphones, the latter usually provide better noise isolation. If you're using your phone to play the recordings, it's advisable to set it to "airplane mode" to prevent its radio transmitter from interfering with your sensitive brainwaves and to avoid interruptions.

I first learned about binaural beats from neurosurgeon Eben Alexander, the author of *Living in a Mindful Universe*. He has a website called "Sacred Acoustics," where you can download free binaural beat recordings to try out.

Chapter 23

INTENSE PAIN

As we've already seen, there is an important distinction between pain and suffering. Pain is a sensation that occurs in the body, while suffering is an experience of the mind. Physical pain may be unavoidable at times, but you can choose how your mind responds to it. When you are in intense pain, you may want to withdraw from your body and retreat into your mind, but this often exacerbates the situation since the stories your mind can attach to the sensation of pain can create a level of suffering that greatly surpasses the discomfort in your body. When you learn to experience the sensation without the story, your suffering will diminish.

As we discussed earlier, physical and emotional pain activate similar areas of the brain, so it makes sense to handle them in similar ways. As mentioned, the way to manage all kinds of pain—whether physical or emotional—is to shift your attention from your thoughts to your body. *This means turning toward the pain instead of away from it.* This practice helps slow your mind and reduce suffering. This applies to all sources of pain, including injuries, illnesses, disabilities, abuse, and other forms of trauma.

I am grateful to have been free from physical pain for many years; however, I still experience occasional migraines, especially if I eat certain foods or engage in specific sports during hot weather. One of those sports is riding a dirt bike in the rocky woods of New England. I sometimes participate in timekeeping competitions known as enduros. Most enduro riders will tell you that the sport is a mix of pleasure and pain. The pleasure comes from the nearly transcendent experience of navigating a narrow, winding trail through the trees. The pain involves handling a 250-pound machine over slippery boulders, fallen trees, deep ruts, and steep ledges for four to five hours, often in hot weather, which can lead to dehydration and exhaustion. Additionally, the pressure of a snug-fitting helmet can cause the blood vessels in my forehead to visibly dilate, sometimes triggering a migraine.

I have learned that a migraine is my body's way of telling me to stop what I'm doing and relax. If I ignore this warning, I will pay a heavy price. That's why I've come to listen to my body and limit my riding to less than three hours, especially when it's hot and the terrain is particularly challenging.

In the summer of 2023, I participated in a competitive off-road motorcycle enduro in Rhode Island. The goal of the event was to maintain a specific average speed between designated checkpoints in the woods. Although I often take part in these events, I usually don't complete the entire course due to the risk of migraines. In this case, I planned to exit at the forty-mile mark and return to the start, which I felt would be enough "fun" for me.

Unfortunately, I missed a turn before the planned bailout point and ended up taking a detour down a section of trail meant for the last part of the race. I realized my mistake over a mile into that section. One of the cardinal rules in enduros is that you should never double back on the course, as it could lead to a head-on collision. This left me with no choice but to continue forward.

It was extremely hot, and I soon felt the early signs of a migraine. I paused to take my rescue medication, which I always carry, drank some electrolyte water mix, and reviewed my map to assess my options. My heart sank when I realized I was on a six-mile stretch of a very slow and challenging trail with no exit points. I would have to travel the next six miles and hope to return to the start before I became too ill.

It took ninety minutes of crawling over large rocks in first gear, and I stumbled and fell several times as the migraine pain steadily worsened. I felt weak and nauseous. I didn't cross paths with any of the other riders because I was far ahead of everyone, having made an incorrect turn early in the race.

By the time I returned to the start, my migraine had intensified, leaving me feeling delirious and nauseous. It felt as if a baseball bat had struck my head, and I struggled to walk. One event organizer saw me crawling into my truck and approached to check on me. I explained what had happened and that I was experiencing a severe migraine. He sympathized and offered consolation, telling me that other riders had also reported poor directions at that turn and nearly made the same mistake. Once in the truck, I started the engine, turned on the air conditioner, and reclined the seat. I began to breathe rapidly, which sometimes helps alleviate my nausea, and took another pill, trying hard to keep it down.

Next, my mind began to attach stories to the pain, such as: Why was I born with this terrible condition? Why is this not happening to anyone else? Why can't I have more fun? When is this going to end? Will I be here all night? I hope nobody sees me like this—and so forth.

My experience taught me that these stories only intensified the suffering and that I needed to stop feeding it with those thoughts. I knew I couldn't be comfortable with this kind of pain, but I leaned into it anyway. Each time a new story emerged in my mind, I shifted my attention back to the pain and faced the fire.

After repeating this several times, I was able to stay relaxed despite the pain. I lay in my truck for the next two hours, maintaining my relaxed attention on the pain instead of attaching stories to it. Gradually, the pain subsided enough for me to drive home. It wasn't a fun experience, but my mind could have made it much worse. In the process, I grew a little bit in "presence power."

It's natural to resist pain and tense up because you fear it will overwhelm you if you relax—but this is not the case. When you relax into pain and don't fight against it, you may notice that it shifts slightly and changes in intensity. These subtle movements create small spaces, and within these spaces, you can find brief moments of partial relief. These spaces resemble those that arise when you relax into emotional pain, but in the case of intense physical pain, these spaces are very subtle.

As stated earlier, our greatest strength often lies hidden within our weaknesses. My predisposition toward migraines is like having a teacher who follows me everywhere, constantly reminding me to relax and not to take life too seriously. Practicing this has significantly reduced the frequency of migraines in my life. Unavoidable, and thankfully rare events like this enduro mishap serve as a harsh reminder of the consequences and a new lesson in the futility of resistance.

The false self is built on resistance—therefore, when you willingly face physical or emotional pain and accept the unacceptable, the false self diminishes. The same applies to any impairment or affliction you must face. Each time the false self lessens, your true self has room to expand, allowing you to grow spiritually.

The most extreme suffering, limitation, and helplessness that a human being can face is far worse than migraine, and is symbolized by the cross. The ancient Romans used it as a torture device, so it's strange that it's become a sacred symbol rather than a horrifying evil. In fact, the cross didn't appear in Christian art and artifacts until the reign of Emperor Constantine in the 300s AD. For the first three hundred years of the church, Christians used the image of fish, doves, and even boat anchors—but never the cross.[47] However, over time, it became clear that the cross has a hidden face: the face of surrender, non-resistance, and acceptance of the unacceptable. This is evident in Christ's prayer in Gethsemane; while expressing his natural desire to avoid the cross, it also highlights his acceptance and surrender, stating, "…*if thou be willing, remove this cup from me: nevertheless not my will, but thine, be done.*"[48]

---

47. https://www.micahbales.com/cross-christian-symbol/ retrieved 5/28/25
48. Lu 22:42

Chapter 24

GOING DEEP

I've always been interested in religious apologetics, which is the study of evidence for the existence of the Divine. This evidence consists of logical arguments for the extreme precision and balance of the universe's physical constants, the intelligent design evident in living things, historical evidence of miracles, and astonishing discoveries in quantum physics that reveal the basis of the material world to be a non-material realm. I have an extensive collection of books on these subjects and consider myself somewhat of an expert. However, I have learned through suffering that the most convincing evidence is found by looking within. What is found within is self-authenticating and needs no argument or external proof.

I discovered that a quiet mind reveals an inner space that is not dull or empty but expansive, comforting, and a source of guidance. Abiding in this quiet space is transformative, and there are no limits to the changes it can bring. Within this peaceful space, there exists an uncaused joy and love that defy natural explanation, as they have nothing to do with thinking or processing what's happening outside of me. It seems logical that peace would come from a quiet mind, and perhaps some joy from escaping the tyranny of the mind; however, it is puzzling to consider why *love* would emerge from stillness. This makes little logical sense. Even more mystifying is the observation that these feelings—peace, joy, and love—are not separate from one another but coexist as a single feeling with multiple dimensions. I believe these unique and beautiful feelings, beyond thought and emotion, are the fruit of our union with the Divine.

Any discussion about the Divine inevitably raises questions about the meaning of life. No explanation can ever be adequate, but the question of whether meaning exists carries profound implications.

The meaning of life is nothing more than a joke to many, and for some great thinkers, like Leo Tolstoy—it is a stupid and evil joke.[49] This perspective arises because natural disasters and the indiscriminate suffering all around us suggest there is no meaning. People are tortured, raped, and murdered every day, and we know that it shouldn't be this way. When we observe the beauty of nature, we see everything trying to eat everything else, which also seems meaningless. We're taught to romanticize the circle of life, but the circle of life is also the circle of death. The Old Testament prophet Solomon was familiar with every pleasure and privilege the world had to offer; yet, he declared them all meaningless because they are fleeting.[50] Perhaps we are just meaningless, transitory blobs of protoplasm—products of chance and time—and nothing really matters. But how could a meaningless world give rise to beings who are aware of its meaninglessness? C.S. Lewis explored this idea with an argument that I will paraphrase:

> *The universe often seems cruel and unfair. But where do we get our ideas of cruelty, fairness, and unfairness? A person cannot label a line as crooked unless they have a concept of a straight line to compare it to. What are we using as a standard when we declare the universe to be cruel or unfair? If the universe is truly senseless from beginning to end, how can we—as part of the universe—feel qualified to judge it? If the universe truly had no meaning, we would not be able to recognize its lack of meaning.*[51]

That argument may not be entirely satisfying, as it does not reveal the meaning of life—something that no one can fully comprehend. However, it suggests that there is a standard of meaning within us. If there is meaning within us, then we cannot be random blobs of protoplasm, because that would be meaningless. Therefore, there must be some aspect of our being that transcends our transitory bodies and fleeting thoughts and emotions. There must be some part of us that is eternal.

---

49. Tolstoy, Confession, p 29
50. Ecclesiastes 9:1-18
51. C.S. Lewis, Mere Christianity, p 61

But if we are eternal beings with some meaning to life, why is the world such a mess? Are we part of some Divine game that is out of control or designed to make everyone miserable? Why isn't the world arranged so that we can all have a great time? It's natural to view the world as a playground and expect it to always make us happy, but what if it's not meant to be a playground? What if it's meant to be a proving ground instead?

A proving ground is a place filled with challenges designed to enhance something. I design mission-critical electronic products that undergo rigorous testing in a proving ground, facilitating necessary improvements. These tests may include exposure to extreme heat and cold, intense vibration, and intentional drops onto hard surfaces. They are essential to the process of developing a successful product.

If the world is a proving ground that is crafted for your growth, life will not always be fun and easy—*proving grounds are inherently messy places*. However, you can have beautiful experiences, but they will not come from outside you—they will arise from within. While we may enjoy pleasant experiences in the world, that good feeling does not last. A pleasant experience is quickly forgotten, leading us to yearn for the next one in our endless pursuit of unobtanium. The spiritual person, however, understands that the most fulfilling experiences come from a deep place within, regardless of what is happening in the messy outside world. Perhaps this world has been crafted to teach us to look inward rather than outward. Maybe that is why Christ taught his disciples that *"the Kingdom of God is within you."*[52]

Looking inward is common to both spirituality and psychology, but they differ in their perspectives on suffering. Psychologists aim to end suffering as quickly as possible by any means necessary, while the spiritual teacher understands that suffering serves a purpose—*it highlights areas where we need to grow.* Anthony de Mello, a priest *and* psychologist, recognized this tension in his work and found that, as a psychotherapist, he was only providing relief rather than cures. He

---

52. Lu 17:21

believed that sometimes people need to hit rock bottom before they can find the cure.[53]

As we have seen, suffering originates in the mind, and mental anguish can serve as a wake-up call—*sweet dreams seldom wake people up; it's the nightmares that do.* For many, it's necessary to reach a point where they are sick and tired of the relentless voice in their head that worries about the future, fixates on the past, clings to attachments, seeks to impress others, and insists that life should be a certain way. When you finally reach your limit with this inner chatter, you become ready to let it go.

Suffering serves as an invitation for introspection and self-examination. While pleasant experiences may provide temporary happiness, they rarely cause us to look inward. Suffering acts as a guide, illuminating areas within us that have not yet matured. It reveals where our illusions clash with reality, and it can be quite painful to witness the shattering of those illusions. Ultimately, suffering increases our awareness of where we need to grow and transform into higher beings.

Whenever I experience suffering, I review the "suffering checklist" below. This set of questions, based on what we've discussed in earlier chapters, often reveals what's blocking growth.

Fortune Telling (worry)

- Am I taking the voice in my head too seriously?

- Have I forgotten that feelings are NOT facts?

- Have I forgotten to attend to the anxious sensations in my body instead of the stories in my head?

- Am I unwilling to surrender by accepting all potential outcomes?

Attachments

- Am I attached to a material thing?

- Have I identified with my job or career?

---

53. Anthony De Mello, Awareness, p 12

- Am I trying to get something from a relationship rather than serving out of love?

Mental Filters

- Am I comparing my life to someone else's life?
- Am I thankful for all the good in my life?
- Am I holding onto a belief that was given to me and isn't truly mine?
- Am I holding onto a false belief?
- Do I feel the need to be right and prove others wrong?

The Past

- Is there something from the past I need to let go?
- Am I listening to the voice of self-doubt and taking it seriously?
- Am I holding onto a grudge or guilt?
- Am I struggling with criticism?
- Am I disappointed with the present because I'm clinging to the past?

Perfectionism

- Is there something imperfect that I need to accept?
- Am I amplifying a minor problem?
- Am I labeling and judging another person who doesn't meet my standards?
- Am I using "should" statements?
- Is my self-talk harsh?

Mind Reading

- Am I imagining what others think or say about me?
- Do I care about what others think?

An *extreme* period of suffering that leads to growth has been described as "The Dark Night of the Soul," a concept captured in a famous poem by St. John of the Cross. The Dark Night is experienced as a feeling of depression, which is the result of reality clashing with a false belief, such as "bad things don't happen to good people." A natural disaster, the premature death of a child, or any sudden and unexpected loss could trigger this. There's a collapse of old beliefs, mental structures, and attachments. Life no longer makes sense during the Dark Night, and its perceived meaning is lost.

To emerge from the depression of the Dark Night, one must see that there is no meaning in this world, and that lasting meaning is found by transcending the world—which means looking within. Any search for lasting meaning in this world will eventually lead to the Dark Night experience, which may happen more than once. Those who emerge from "The Dark Night of the Soul" have a new perspective and have grown into higher beings. They are *in* the world, but are no longer *of* the world, and in fact, they have overcome the world.[54]

The Dark Night is not something to fear; rather, the only thing to truly fear is staying asleep and not awakening to discover your true self. Like all seasons of life, the Dark Night is temporary, and it will eventually pass. If you allow the Dark Night to fulfill its purpose, it will strip away all illusions, enabling you to see what is real and enduring—your true self. Many individuals have emerged from the Dark Night with newfound clarity, peace, and joy.

Many situations in life can be changed to avoid suffering, and there's nothing wrong with that. We should strive to alleviate suffering by taking action whenever possible, while also engaging in self-reflection and introspection. However, life is full of challenging situations that *cannot* be changed—*unchangeable situations offer the greatest opportunities for growth.*

One unchangeable fact that almost everyone resists is the death of the body and departing this world. For most people, death is a mental

---

54. Jn 16:33

concept that seems to apply only to others. We acknowledge it intellec-
tually but generally push it away and suppress the thought. Any serious
discussion about death is considered morbid and taboo in our culture.
But if death is an undeniable truth, why not face it and learn to accept
or even welcome its inevitability?

Death reminds us that possessions, careers, and social status mean
nothing beyond the grave, making everyone equal in this way. While
it's okay to enjoy these aspects of life, forming attachments to them
ultimately causes suffering. Searching for meaning in these temporary
things is futile because they are fleeting, and their meaning will be lost
to death. If life is a proving ground, then you should aim to leave this
world as a higher being than when you arrived—*growth is the only thing
you can truly take with you.*

You've probably heard the saying, *"And ye shall know the truth,
and the truth shall make you free."*[55] Death is an undeniable truth, and
accepting that truth will liberate you. When you embrace your death,
you realize that the big problems you worry about now will be trivial in
a relatively short time. Today's major issues appear much smaller when
viewed through this lens, losing their power to bother you. Embracing
death is the ultimate reframing of life, as it allows you to see the bigger
picture. Viewing life in the context of your death is the quintessence
of awareness.

The practice of contemplating your death is known as "die before
you die." Western Massachusetts is home to some very old cemeteries,
hidden in the woods and accessible only by trails. When I ride my dirt
bike there, I enjoy stopping and exploring them. I imagine all the worries
the people buried there once had—*but which no longer matter.* I'm sure
none of them wished they had worried more or collected more stuff.

Reflecting on death serves as a reminder that your time is limited
and should not be wasted on useless and negative thoughts about the
past and future. Instead, focus on the present. By being present, you
can better appreciate simple pleasures and serve others by sharing your

---

55. Jn 8:32

love. Embracing this perspective transforms life into a cherished adventure rather than a series of problems.

Thoughts about death create fear in most people, which is why they are generally pushed away and suppressed. However, fear is suffering, and suffering always points to where growth is needed. Growth is about releasing mental and emotional clutter and uncovering the vast ocean of peace, joy, *and love* that lies beneath. This kind of love cannot coexist with fear—in fact, it drives out all fear because the two are incompatible.

Chapter 25

FEAR AND LOVE

There is no fear in love—*"but perfect love casteth out fear, because fear hath punishment; and he that feareth is not made perfect in love."* [56] In this context, perfect love refers to the unconditional, selfless, and Divine love that transcends thought and emotion, and is found *beneath* your thoughts and emotions. This type of love dispels fear, as fear is often associated with punishment. It is said that all human emotions can be traced back to either a state of love or a state of fear, and if you examine yourself, you will find this to be true. However, human love can sometimes intertwine with fear, such as when you try to love someone out of fear of losing them, or when you try to love God out of fear of punishment. But Divine love and fear cannot coexist, since Divine love always acts as a force to expel fear. As you grow spiritually and separate from the false self—also called the ego, lower self, or sinful nature—you begin to experience the unique and perfect love that lies beyond the mind, and all fear starts to dissolve.

Fear can be deeply ingrained because of past conditioning. Many people with religious backgrounds have been conditioned to fear mental stillness because they were taught it would open them to some false god. However, if there is only one true God—as many believe—then a false god cannot be anything real. *A false god can only be a mental construct.* All mental constructs, and therefore all false gods, will dissolve when the mind is still.

If Divine love can be experienced when the mind is still, then the Divine is more than any mental concept. Mental concepts, such as doctrines and creeds, can serve as helpful pointers, but they do not

---

56. 1 Jn 4:18 ASV

embody reality—*the reality is what they point to*. Once you experience that reality, the doctrines become less significant.

Many religious doctrines imply mental stillness, yet we have been conditioned to view religion primarily as a set of rules. Most religions denounce worry, hatred, anger, judgment, greed, jealousy, and lust, but a moment of reflection makes it clear that these sins are products of the mind. If you are no longer a slave to your mind, you are also free from these sins. Religious texts that condemn these sins—such as the Sermon on the Mount[57]—should be understood as admonitions to quiet the mind rather than as a list of rules to follow. An overemphasis on sin has led many in the modern world to develop a distaste for religion and to "throw the baby out with the bathwater." However, religion holds value because it can raise awareness of the mind's dysfunction and point to the ineffable that lies beyond it.

The dysfunctional mind tends to dwell on the past and the future while resisting the present. The present is never good enough for the mind, so it reminisces about yesterday or wants a better tomorrow. However, when the mind is still, you experience the eternal, timeless present. The fullness of life is found in the timeless present because that's where all of reality happens and where your entire life unfolds. Discovering this timeless place of peace and rest, free from the mental noise of the past and future, is like finding a hidden treasure that becomes precious to you.

Thoughts about a future heaven can be comforting—and this certainly has its place—but they can also create resistance to life. If your thoughts are primarily about "getting out of here" instead of welcoming the challenges of the present, you are resisting life. Resistance leads to stagnation and hinders your growth. *If you are resisting life, then you are missing the whole point of your life—which is to grow.*

It's natural to have numerous questions about heaven and eternity, and the mind craves simple answers. However, reality is always complex and nuanced—*only fairy tales are simple*. Where would you begin

---

57. Mt, chapters 5-7

if you tried to explain to an alien what life is like for a human on planet Earth? The answer is endless, nuanced, and different for each person on this tiny planet, so how much truer is that for life in infinite eternity? Making peace with reality means being comfortable saying "I don't know" instead of pretending your mind has it all figured out. In my experience, the more one grows spiritually, the less one cares about these questions. That said, nearly all spiritual traditions agree on this point—*how you respond to the challenges of this life will determine the path you will follow in the life to come.*

The spiritual path is not about a destination but rather about the journey itself. The mind often views spirituality in a black-and-white manner, labeling people as enlightened or unenlightened, saved or lost, righteous or wicked, and so forth. However, spirituality is not about a transaction, and binary labels do not reflect reality. A few rare individuals have undergone a sudden collapse of the false self; however, for most, the spiritual path is a gradual continuum of growth, accompanied by numerous setbacks. This path is rocky, filled with many ups and downs, twists and turns, making it easy to stumble, stray from the path, and feel lost. However, falling down and feeling lost are essential aspects of this journey—these experiences highlight areas where growth is necessary.

The famous Parable of the Prodigal Son illustrates the cycle of wandering away and then finding your way back.[58] In this parable, a son wanders from home, makes mistakes, and suffers greatly. However, over time, he learns from his errors and decides to return home, where he is welcomed with compassion and joy. This cycle occurs as your mind wanders, you overreact to situations, and then your false self takes control, resulting in mistakes and suffering. Ultimately, you find your way back to a place of rest, where you are centered and aware. Wandering away and returning home—also known as repentance—is not a one-time event. It is a continuous, lifelong process essential for your growth.

---

58. Lu 15:11-32

When embarking on the spiritual path, it's natural to focus on *doing* something or playing the role of a spiritual person—but this is like putting the cart before the horse. Your state of *being*, which is what's going on inside, is more important than what you are *doing* on the outside. If you want to grow genuinely, you must be authentic instead of playing a role that others expect of you. Being authentic is not difficult because it does not require the intense effort of role-playing. Right doing flows out of right being—out of love—and not out of expectations, obligations, or habit. The well-known passage commonly read at weddings expresses this truth:

"And if I bestow all my goods to feed the poor, and if I give my body to be burned, but have not love, it profiteth me nothing." [59]

Life involves making choices and decisions, but the mind often struggles to know what to do. Constantly fluctuating thoughts and emotions cannot be trusted—they will tie you in knots and surround you with a cloud of fear and confusion. However, when the mind is still, the haze will lift, and new light will be revealed. When your state of being is permeated with love, joy, and peace, the necessary actions you need to take will become clear. This is why the Divine within has been called "The Counselor" or "The Comforter." [60] This inner counsel emerges in the form of new awareness, which begins to flow as the mental noise quiets down and programmed reactions dissolve.

It's common to refer to this inner counsel as a "still small voice," but it's more accurately described as a sense of knowing rather than a literal voice. The wavering voice in your head that can't decide what to do is the voice of the false self—this is why listening to voices in your head often leads to trouble. When you hear this voice, it's your cue that it's time to be quiet. By working on quieting this mental noise, you'll gain clarity on what to do in every situation. That's why Mother Teresa taught that "the fruit of silence is prayer." Silence is not a passive state but an active one that connects you with something infinitely greater

---

59. I Co 13:3 ASV
60. Jn 14:16,26

than yourself. This is how you can live out and embody the saying, "Let go and let God." This isn't a doctrine to believe in—it's something to practice and experience for yourself.

Remember that spiritual growth isn't about adding anything to your life; it's about removing or subtracting the obstacles that stand in the way. If the Divine is omnipresent—present everywhere—then you cannot say the Divine is in one person but not another. All you can say is that one person has removed the obstacles to knowing the Divine, while another has not. These obstacles are the sum of the automatic thoughts and reactions of the mind-made false self.

If an obstacle is holding you back, such as an attachment, do not renounce it. When you attempt to renounce something that hinders your growth, you empower what you are trying to reject. Renunciation is a form of resistance, and resistance ultimately leads to persistence. Therefore, if you try to renounce television, it will forever be your master. If you are attached to sports cars and attempt to renounce them, they will always pull you in. Renunciation is not the path to freedom.

Freedom is achieved through awareness, which involves insight and understanding to recognize what holds you back and does not serve you or others. As we saw earlier, awareness is a knowing that goes much deeper than intellectual knowledge. Awareness unveils reality and fosters a distaste for the obstacles that impede your progress. Awareness will lessen your appetite for television and sports cars if they are holding you back. *By simply being aware, everything that holds you back will begin to fall away with little effort.* This includes your attachments, worries, fears, and past experiences.

Awareness often arises after a period of suffering, revealing areas where you need to grow, but that isn't the only way. A more effective approach to generating awareness is to practice daily quiet time and allow life's everyday challenges to be your teacher. Difficult situations are inevitable, but if you've practiced with the smaller challenges, you will discover ways to serve and grow through every experience. As you develop awareness, your false identity will begin to crumble and fall apart, leading to the ultimate demise of the false self, also known as "dying to self."

The false self is rooted in a feeling of separation from others, creating a "me versus them" mentality that hinders growth. When the false self starts to crumble, it becomes clear that this separation is an illusion, because the true self knows we're all connected to one another and the Divine. The word "atonement" describes this connection, which comes from the phrase "at-one-ment," historically carrying at its heart the notion of bringing parties together—unifying or reconciling them.[61]

This connectedness is illustrated by a vine with its many branches, where all people are branches connected to one vine, and each branch draws its life from the vine.[62] Because the vine and branches are one unit, love and service to others are equivalent to love and service to oneself and the Divine. Similarly, if you harm another branch, you're hurting yourself because you're part of the same vine. Branches that try to live in the illusion of separation will wither and become unfruitful because they are cut off from the vine. The false self resides in this disconnected world, which is the basis for all fear. The true self knows its connection to the vine, which creates confidence and a willingness to surrender, and serves as the foundation for faith, hope, and love—but the greatest of these is love.[63]

Connectedness is not a doctrine to believe in—it is known experientially when the false self begins to fade. This happens when you feel unconditional love for someone very different from you, someone you may have previously avoided or even despised. The concept of "loving your neighbor as yourself" may seem illogical to the mind, but it is very real and starts to flow out of you as the false self diminishes.

Connectedness is also known through surrendering to the flow of life and not demanding specific outcomes. Surrender teaches you that the moment you are experiencing now is not solely about you, but instead that you are a participant in a much larger dance that began eons ago. Although this dance includes situations you label as good or bad, you eventually come to realize how everything works together

---

61. https://plato.stanford.edu/archives/sum2023/entries/atonement/ retrieved 5/28/25
62. Jn 15:5
63. I Co 13:13

for your good, facilitating your growth.[64] This dance does not center around you, but you have the privilege of participating in a small way. No single atom in the universe is separate from you; each has played a tiny role in a cascade of events that started fourteen billion years ago and has brought you to this unique moment. This realization is both humbling and awe-inspiring.

When the illusion of separation dissolves, serving others becomes natural as your desires transform. This higher state of being has been called the "absence of desire," but I think it's more accurately described as the "absence of want" because you *will desire* to share your love, rather than wanting to fill some emotional need. You *will desire* to let go of attachments, not as renunciation, but because you've developed new tastes for something better. When doing flows out of being, your service will be motivated by love rather than duty or obligation.

Instead of trying to serve others in a big way, just notice the little opportunities around you each moment. Just as the simplest moments bring the greatest pleasures, the simplest acts of kindness can have the most profound impact. Mahatma Gandhi said, "The simplest acts of kindness are by far more powerful than a thousand heads bowing in prayer." This means pausing to listen to someone who is hurting instead of offering advice, chatting with an elderly neighbor who lives alone, smiling at someone you pass every day, complimenting someone, doing a simple chore when you haven't been asked, or picking up a nail so that someone you will never meet avoids a flat tire.

The little choices we make each moment create lasting change. Every time you make a choice, you are transforming the highest part of you—the part that chooses—into something slightly different from what it was before. Everyday choices that may seem trivial hold tremendous significance because they transform not only us, but also those around us. Once we recognize this, boredom and malaise give way to enthusiasm and a zest for life.

---

64. Ro 8:28

There is no substitute for experiential knowledge, which is why you are on this planet. Classroom learning, sermons, and reading books can provide head knowledge, but real knowing and real growth occur when you navigate the ups and downs of real life. Some experiences on this planet are pleasant, while others are not so pleasant, but all have been crafted for your growth, so it's best not to resist them. Every experience should be accepted, so that your true self can mature into something a little different and a little better, enabling you to leave this world as a higher being than when you arrived.

If you continually ask yourself, "Who am I?" you *will* grow into a higher being. Each time an unwelcome thought or feeling tries to take hold of you, remember that it is not who you truly are. Then, relax and create some space so it can pass through you. Keep your attention on the sensations in your body instead of the stories in your head to quiet your mind and release emotional energy. Please don't wait for a crisis to begin this practice—work with the small challenges that happen daily. By doing so, you will experience life's richness on a profound level without getting stuck in pain. You will stop expecting the outside world to make you happy, and your life will become an adventure instead of a series of problems. You can achieve this, and there are no limits to your growth or the impact you can have on the world. The fact that you've made it this far shows that your journey of growth has already begun, and I admire you for that.

With great love and admiration,

James Garrett

Appendix A

COGNITIVE BEHAVIORAL THERAPY (CBT)

Cognitive behavioral therapy (CBT) is a type of psychological treatment that has proven effective for various issues, including depression, anxiety disorders, alcohol and drug use problems, marital issues, eating disorders, and severe mental illness. Numerous research studies indicate that CBT significantly enhances functioning and quality of life. In many studies, it is as effective as, or more effective than, other forms of psychological therapy or psychiatric medications.[65] Many excellent books on CBT are available, such as *Feeling Good* by Dr. David Burns. An in-depth discussion of CBT is beyond the scope of this book; however, I would like to give you, the reader, a taste of what's involved.

I've incorporated many aspects of CBT into this book, including expressive writing and awareness of various types of erroneous thinking. In CBT, erroneous thoughts are referred to as cognitive distortions, typically encompassing ten distinct types. If you've made it this far, you should be familiar with most of them, which I've summarized below.

1. **Jumping to Conclusions**

   a. Fortune Telling - Worrying.

   b. Mind Reading - Imagining what others think about you.

2. **Catastrophizing** - Turning minor situations into catastrophes (aka amplification).

---

65. https://pmc.ncbi.nlm.nih.gov/articles/PMC3563285/ retrieved 5/28/25

3. **Mental Filters** – Seeing only the negative, and failing to see the big picture.

4. **Perfectionism** - If anything isn't perfect, it's all wrong (aka all-or-nothing thinking).

5. **Dismissing the Positive** – Discounting compliments from others

6. **Should Statements** - Judging the world and others according to your standards.

7. **Overgeneralization** – Always and never statements, such as I *always* lose and things *never* go right

8. **Labeling** - Extreme overgeneralization, such as I'm an idiot, I'm stupid, I'm a fool.

9. **Emotional Reasoning** – Assuming that feelings are facts, as in I feel worthless, therefore I am worthless.

10. **Personalization** – Taking responsibility for what someone else did.

Expressive writing is foundational to CBT and has played a pivotal role in my healing journey. We've already discussed expressive writing, but some key points are worth reviewing. This is not journaling or keeping a diary, and it requires no special skills or techniques. I often use the term "expressive scribbling" because it must be uninhibited and done without paying attention to form, grammar, punctuation, spelling, neatness, or content. You should feel free to scribble out your most private and uncomfortable thoughts and feelings, and then rip them up when you're done.

You might not want to do this if you're a man. Despite evidence of its effectiveness, I resisted expressive writing for over a year. Your mind may convince you it's a waste of time, foolish, or too feminine, but you need to do it anyway. As I've stated, if you don't do anything else you've read about in this book, I urge you to commit to this one practice twice a day for at least a few weeks.

More than 200 papers demonstrate the efficacy of expressive writing. It is 85 percent effective in improving or resolving anxiety, and I can testify that it works even if you don't believe in it. There is no debate about its effectiveness; the only discussion is about why it works.

Writing by hand uniquely engages your brain and differs from typing on a computer, although that can be beneficial as well. This complex task activates large areas of the brain, translating thoughts into motor functions.

Expressive writing is the quickest and most effective way to begin separating from your thoughts and has been called "mechanical meditation." If you're unsure what to write, just write that. If you think it's a pointless waste of time, write it down. If you're in severe pain, write about it. If something is bothering you, jot it down. If you're happy about something, write about that. It doesn't matter whether you focus on positive or negative experiences. Whatever thoughts, whether they are nonsense or sense, are in your mind, put them on paper.

Once you become comfortable with jotting down your thoughts, you can take the next step in CBT, which is to review what you've written and categorize each thought. One way to do this is to divide a piece of paper into three columns.[66] In the first column, write the thought; in the second column, note the type of cognitive distortion it represents; and in the third column, write the action you may need to take. You can cross out the items over which you have no control and where no possible action can be taken. For example, if you've observed someone driving dangerously, you may express a should statement like "they should not drive like that," but there is no action to take other than accepting it. For those that may require some action, but none that you can take today, write out a plan for what you will do in the future, and then let those items go.

Some thoughts can be categorized under multiple headings. For me, perfectionism, catastrophizing, labeling, and fortune-telling often converge in a single thought, such as: "I'm an idiot for getting a drop of paint on the carpet; now it's completely ruined, and my wife is going to kill me." That single thought encompasses four categories.

---

66. Burns, Feeling Good, p 7

The following is an example of the three-column technique. I've added two categories, "Attachments" and "The Past," that are not part of secular CBT but have a place in spiritual growth.

Thought	Cognitive Distortion	Corrective Action
Everyone must think I'm weird.	Mind Reading	I don't really know what others are thinking, and they're probably not thinking about me at all. I will let this go and cross it out.
Tomorrow is going to be a disaster.	Fortune Telling	I am predicting a terrible future that exists only in my head. I will let this go and cross it out.
People should be more considerate.	Should Statements	The world is full of inconsiderate people whom I cannot change. I will accept this fact, let it go, and cross it out.
I made a mistake—I'm such an idiot.	Labeling	I'm going to start talking to myself the same way I would speak to my own children.
I lost my favorite pen. I'm so upset I can't concentrate on my work.	Catastrophizing	I will say out loud, "This is a very small problem—it's just a pen."
That dent in my truck is really bugging me—this truck is no good now, and I hate driving it.	Perfectionism	I'll call the Dent Wizard, get it fixed, and let it go.
I never do anything right	Over-generalization	I'll change my self-talk to match reality—"I sometimes make mistakes and that's OK."

My adult child is making bad choices, and it's my fault.	Personalization	My child is an adult and must make his own decisions—I'm letting this go.
I feel useless and worthless; therefore, I am useless and worthless.	Emotional Reasoning	Feelings are NOT facts. I'm letting this thinking go.
All my neighbors seem to be doing well, but my life is a complete mess.	Mental Filters	I'm going to stop comparing my life to everyone else's and be thankful for what I have.
This restaurant was fantastic the last time I was here, but for some reason, it feels different, and I can't enjoy myself.	The Past	I'm not going to cling to past experiences (good or bad) and enjoy what is happening in the present.
I must have that new BMW and cannot be happy until it's in my driveway.	Attachments	Happiness does not come from anything outside of me—I'm letting this thought go.

Appendix B

CHUNG-JANSEN SYNDROME

My son Ayden was diagnosed with Chung-Jansen Syndrome (CJS) at the age of 20. Before his diagnosis, we had no idea what was wrong with him, as this syndrome was only identified in 2018. Currently, there are only about 400 known cases, but that number is increasing as more people undergo genetic testing. Although CJS is considered rare, its true prevalence remains unknown, and it is likely to have existed for centuries. I share this information to raise awareness about the disorder and to hopefully support other families facing similar challenges.

CJS, also known as PHIP disorder, is a genetic condition caused by mutations in the PHIP gene. It is linked to widespread developmental delays, which may include difficulties with early walking, talking, and fine motor skills. Additionally, individuals with CJS may experience varying degrees of intellectual disability, anxiety, and behavioral challenges. The PHIP gene mutation typically happens spontaneously and is not inherited from either parent. However, in some cases, the mutation can be inherited, leading to a 50% chance of a child inheriting CJS from an affected parent.

Behavioral problems are a significant characteristic of CJS. Many children with CJS exhibit oppositional, defiant, and aggressive behaviors, often diagnosed as oppositional defiant disorder (ODD). These children can become easily angered and experience mood swings. They frequently struggle to regulate their emotions, leading to tantrums that can occur easily and last for extended periods of time. Managing this behavior can be challenging for parents and siblings, and difficulties may also arise in school or other settings.

Many children and adults with CJS exhibit autistic features. Although they are not always diagnosed with autism, their behaviors often suggest it. Many parents utilize methods designed for individuals with autism, such as providing a safe and highly structured environment.

Attention-deficit/hyperactivity disorder (ADHD) is common in CJS, manifesting as difficulty concentrating and sometimes hyperactive and impulsive behaviors. For these children, sitting still in class or completing tasks independently can be difficult because they tend to become easily distracted.

Sensory processing can be abnormal among individuals with CJS, leading to inappropriate responses to certain stimuli. Many individuals may become oversensitive to specific textures and sounds. They often experience hypersensitivity in crowded environments, which is why headphones or earplugs are commonly used to help manage these reactions.

Individuals with CJS often exhibit distinctive facial features, such as a broad forehead, thick eyebrows, an upturned nose, large ears with prominent earlobes, and a round face. Many of these individuals may struggle with weight management, particularly as they age. Additional physical characteristics may include low muscle tone, vision problems, gastrointestinal issues, and abnormalities in finger and toe development, such as webbed toes and crooked fingers.

Developmental Coordination Disorder (DCD) often co-occurs with CJS and is characterized by difficulties in coordination and movement, affecting both fine and gross motor skills. Children with DCD may struggle with tasks such as drawing, writing, dressing themselves, or using utensils like knives and forks. They are often perceived as rigid and may be described as clumsy.

Early diagnosis and timely therapeutic interventions, including speech, physical, and occupational therapy, are crucial for supporting development. Cognitive behavioral therapy (CBT) and other treatments can effectively manage anxiety, improve emotional regulation, and enhance social skills in later life. In some instances, a psychiatrist may prescribe medication to address specific behavioral or emotional issues. The primary focus is on fostering growth and overall well-being.

Joining support groups with other families affected by CJS provides valuable emotional support and practical advice. For more information on the syndrome, please see: https://chungjansensyndrome.eu/en/about-us/

ABOUT THE AUTHOR

James Garrett is a design engineer in the high-tech electronics industry. His work has contributed to the development of specialized equipment used in the financial sector, which is part of a vital global infrastructure. James tackles complex problems at what is often called the "bleeding edge" of technology—the stage just before the "cutting edge." This area frequently involves new and potentially disruptive ideas that can be challenging to navigate.

In addition to his professional pursuits, James enjoys exploring unconventional ideas for personal and spiritual growth while helping others develop. His insights are shaped by his experiences with suffering and the limitations of positive thinking, particularly through the challenges of raising a child with a rare genetic disorder known as Chung-Jansen Syndrome. He also volunteers as a Sunday school teacher and a math tutor in public schools. James is happily married and the father of three adult children, dedicating himself fully to his youngest child, who has special needs.

James places a high value on constructive thinking but recognizes that our minds can sometimes be our worst enemy, leading to physical illness. This insight has led him to foster a strong appreciation for mental stillness and awareness. He is committed to teaching others about the value of stillness and awareness—concepts often overlooked and misunderstood in both secular and sacred educational systems.

In his free time, he enjoys off-road motorcycling, mountain biking, and staying fit. You can contact James at james@mindbodyhurts.com or visit www.mindbodyhurts.com

BIBLIOGRAPHY

- A Grief Observed, C. S. Lewis, 1/20/2006, Blackstone Audio, Inc.
- A New Earth, Eckhart Tolle, 12/26/2004, Penguin Audio
- Aware, Daniel Siegel, M.D., 8/21/2018, Penguin Audio
- Awareness, Anthony de Mello, 10/2/2019, The Center for Spiritual Exchange
- Back in Control, 2nd Edition, Dr. David Hanscom,5/16/2017, Vertus Press
- Becoming Nobody, Ram Dass, 9/3/2019, Sounds True
- Breathing, Andrew Weil, MD,1/2/2001, Sounds True
- Change Your Mind, RJ Spina, 8/8/2023, Llewellyn Publications
- Christian History Made Easy, Timothy Paul Jones, 7/19/1999, Rose Pub Inc
- Confession, Leo Tolstoy, David Patterson, W. W. Norton & Co., 1983
- Fearlessness, Anthony De Mello, 12/7/2023, Center for Spiritual Exchange
- Feeling Good, David D. Burns, MD, 3/21/2017, HarperAudio
- Freedom Through Higher Awareness, Dr. Wayne W. Dyer, 10/14/2014, Nightingale-Conant
- Fulfilled, Anna Yusim, Eben Alexander, 6/27/2017, Hachette Audio
- Healing Back Pain, John E. Sarno, M.D., 7/27/2001, Macmillan Audio
- How to Be a No-Limit Person, Dr. Wayne W. Dyer,10/14/2014, Nightingale-Conant

- Imagine That, James Mapes, 10/4/2016, Greenleaf Book Group Press

- I'm Right, You're Wrong, Now What?, Xavier Amador, 4/1/2008, Balance

- Infinite Potential, Lothar Schäfer, Deepak Chopra, 4/2/2013, Random House Audio

- Inner Engineering, Jaggi Vasudev–Sadhguru, 2/1/2018, Sounds True

- Karma, Sadhguru, 4/27/2021, Random House Audio

- Letting Go, David R. Hawkins, MD/PHD, 12/28/2014, Hay House LLC

- Letting Go of Nothing, Peter Russell, Eckhart Tolle, 11/10/2021, Recorded Books, Inc.

- Light From Light, Louis Dupre, James Wiseman, 5/1/2021, Paulist Press

- Living from a Place of Surrender, Michael A. Singer, 10/1/2019, Sounds True

- Living in a Mindful Universe, Eben Alexander, MD, Karen Newell, 10/17/2017, Brilliance Audio

- Living Untethered, Michael A. Singer, 5/10/2022, Tantor Audio

- Man's Search for Meaning, Viktor E. Frankl

- Marcus Aurelius–Meditations, Marcus Aurelius, James Harris, 11/24/2016, James Harris

- Mere Christianity, C. S. Lewis, 12/26/2004, Blackstone Audio, Inc.

- Sadhana, Anthony de Mello, 9/22/2022, Center for Spiritual Exchange

- Self-Healing with Sound & Music, Andrew Weil, Kimba Arem, 10/6/2015, Sounds True

- Sleep Smarter, Shawn Stevenson, Sara Gottfried, MD, 8/16/2016, Audible Studios

- Stillness Speaks, Eckhart Tolle, 8/1/2003, New World Library

- Stop Fixing Yourself, Anthony De Mello, 9/21/2021, Tantor Audio
- The Great Pain Deception, Steve Ozanich, 12/13/2011
- The Language of God, Francis Collins, 7/17/2007,
- The Language of Science and Faith, Karl Giverson, Francis Collins, 2/15/2011, IVP
- The Magic of Awareness, Anam Thubten, Sharon Roe, 12/9/2014, Audible Studios
- The Mindbody Prescription, John E. Sarno, M.D., 1/17/2012, Hachette Audio
- The Power of Now, Eckhart Tolle, 12/31/2000, New World Library
- The Problem of Pain, C.S. Lewis, 4/28/2015, HarperOne
- The Scalpel and the Soul, Allan Hamilton, 4/2/2009, Tarcher
- The Sin of Certainty, Peter Enns, 1/1/1986, Tantor Media Inc
- The Surrender Experiment, Michael A. Singer, 6/2/2015, Random House Audio
- The Ultimate Deepak Chopra, Deepak Chopra MD, 10/14/2014, Nightingale-Conant
- The Universe Always Has a Plan, Matt Kahn, 3/24/2020, Hay House LLC
- The Untethered Soul, Michael A. Singer, 12/12/2011, Tantor Audio
- The Way to Love, Anthony de Mello, 4/19/2020, The Center for Spiritual Exchange
- Think Away Your Pain, David Schechter, M.D., 9/21/2016, Mind-Body Medicine Publications
- True Discipleship, William MacDonald, 6/6/2003, Gospel Folio Press
- To Be or Not To Be Pain Free, Marc Sopher, 2/1/2003, 1st Book Library

- Understanding Is the New Healing, Dr. Mary Helen Hensley, 1/29/2021, Dr. Mary Helen Hensley
- Wayne Dyer's Ultimate Library, Dr. Wayne W. Dyer, 10/31/2017, Nightingale-Conant
- Wellsprings, Anthony de Mello, 9/27/2022, Center for Spiritual Exchange
- Why I Am a Christian, John Stott, 12/03/2003, IVP Books
- You Are Here, Gabrielle Bernstein, 4/20/2020, Audible Originals
- Your Body Is Your Subconscious Mind, Candace Pert, 11/2/2005, Sounds True

www.ingramcontent.com/pod-product-compliance
Lightning Source LLC
LaVergne TN
LVHW051047080426
835508LV00019B/1748